Understanding
THE BRITISH COUNTRYSIDE

AUTHOR'S NOTE

After many months in preparation, this book finally went to press on February 14 2001. Just one week later a case of foot and mouth disease was discovered at an abattoir in Essex, being the first outbreak on mainland Britain for over 30 years. The scale of this dreadful occurrence is still unfolding as the book is being bound and completed and has been widely covered in the media. The brief passing mention given to the disease on page 71 is now quite inadequate but indicates perhaps just how totally unexpected and almost unprecedented these recent events have been.

Peter A B Prag
March 2001

Understanding THE BRITISH COUNTRYSIDE

PETER A B PRAG
MA FRICS

Foreword by Frederick Forsyth CBE

Estates gazette

First published in 2001 by
Estates Gazette
151 Wardour Street, London W1F 8BN

in association with
Farmers Weekly and NFU Countryside

ISBN 0 7282 0353 7

Typesetting and design by Ted Masters

Printed in Great Britain by
The Manson Group

FOREWORD

We British, I often think, are a very strange people. We tend to elevate to rank, fortune and popular adoration things and people that are, at root, cheap, shallow, passing temporary, fashionable, modish or merely trendy.

Yet when we have something that has deep and lasting value, something that took years, even centuries, of hard toil by our ancestors to create, we treat that thing with contempt, or with apathy and ignorance, which is almost the same thing.

Then, if one day we lose it and realise too late how valuable and perhaps irreplaceable it was, the cry goes up that 'someone' should have done something to prevent the loss.

As I write at the start of the year 2001, Britain is in a state of social and constitutional flux such as I have never seen. Everything we have that seemed in my young manhood to be immutable is under assault – the headship of state, parliament, democracy, national self-governance.

One of our national treasures, which took centuries of labour and no little loving care to produce is the countryside, which I happen to deem the most beautiful of Europe. Yet the people of that countryside are as seldom before in a mood of exasperation and even anger, believing themselves and their landscape, their economy and traditions to be also among those things subjected to criticism and assault. Why should this be and is it true?

Here we run into a strange dichotomy. In a country where now less than 20% of the population can truly be described as 'rural', and thus over 80% must dwell in the city, town or suburb, the polls yet show that 80% of the British avow they appreciate the countryside. By anyone's arithmetic that must mean that three quarters of townspeople believe they really appreciate the rural landscape.

PREFACE

Peers of Organic Farmers and Growers Ltd, Mark Bacon, Charles Sands and Teresa Wickham of TWA Communications.

The countryside is not only complex but also of course very beautiful and I am delighted therefore to have been able to include so many illustrations. A large number of the photographs were sourced from Farmers Weekly but I am grateful also to the following for providing individual pictures: AGCO Ltd (Massey Ferguson) (pages 31 & 36), Blue Circle Industries plc (page 164), Country Life Picture Library (page 144), Humberts (pages 139 & 173), John Clegg & Co. (pages 109, 119 & 121), John Deere Ltd (pages 21 & 34), McConnel Ltd (page 66) and Yvonne Toms (page 1).

In any household it is already more than enough if one person is engaged in producing a book and I tried to shield my wife from the trials and tribulations that it involves. Happily, however, I failed to do so and Sue has been a marvellous source of enthusiasm, encouragement and advice. She even suffered herself to read through the entire manuscript and it became much the better for that.

Peter A B Prag
February 2001

CONTENTS

CONTENTS

CONTENTS

1 INTRODUCTION

It has often been said that the landscape of Britain has been largely created by humans and that however natural and beautiful some of it may appear to be, there are in fact only very few places where the present scenery has not been influenced by farming and forestry practices carried out across the ages. But the way in which these practices evolved, particularly in recent times, is very much bound up in the natural and inescapable phenomena of our geography and climate. The western side of the country enjoys (or perhaps suffers!) a greater amount of rainfall than the east, being the place where the Atlantic airstreams first meet land. It is also in the west that most of the higher ground is found. This steeper ground not only adds to the impact of the rain-bearing airstreams but also can be difficult or impossible to cultivate. In the east, on the other hand, most of the land is lower lying and relatively level. In a farming context, this drier and more even ground provides better conditions for arable cropping, especially the staple cereals of wheat and barley. Not only is it easier to harvest when there is a lesser risk of rain, but the land is also easier to cultivate at times of ploughing or sowing. The lesser rainfall and potentially lighter soils mean, however, that grass would not grow as well as in the west where the wetter conditions can produce more abundant growth.

1 INTRODUCTION

Our present-day landscape largely reflects these underlying circumstances, with grassland predominating in the west and arable land to the east, although this was not always the case and there are still notable exceptions. For example, under the lee of the Welsh hills which comprise some of the steepest and wettest areas in southern Britain, lie the rich red soils of Herefordshire and Shropshire that are famed for their arable crops. In Cornwall too, despite being in the front line of the Atlantic weather, land is used successfully for the cultivation of potatoes and other vegetable crops, in this case to exploit the fact that the southerly climate allows for an earlier harvest and thus an economic advantage over much of the rest of the country. Generally, however, one is more likely to associate Cornwall with cream, and therefore grazing for cows, and an area such as East Anglia with the wide vistas of wheat and barley.

Such specialisation really only became possible with the advent of artificial fertilisers and pesticides and improved transportation. Traditionally, farms in what are now arable areas would have had to carry some livestock. This was in order to provide manure that was essential for fertility, as well as a break from arable cropping to reduce the incidence of disease. There was, furthermore, a need to have a local supply of milk and meat in the days before railways or metalled roads. In the western regions, on the other hand, farmers would have persevered with cereal cropping alongside their pastures in order to provide essential winter feed for the livestock, in addition to relying only on hay. Nowadays arable farming can be sustained without animal manure, while meat, milk and other perishable products can be transported swiftly and safely around the country. Animal feedstuffs can also be brought in from outside and hay is being supplemented or surpassed by silage, which is a more efficient form of conserved forage and slightly less dependent on fine weather at harvest. Nonetheless, there are still occasional signs of the more mixed agricultural countryside of earlier days, such as disused cattle yards in the eastern counties or old granaries on dairy farms or indeed trees standing within open arable fields where hedges would once have been.

1 INTRODUCTION

Our woods and forests are also part of this geographic evolution. Britain was once thickly wooded, but over the centuries land has been cleared to make way for farming and to provide for fuel and building materials. Now, there are fewer woods remaining in the east of the country and more seem to have been retained in the south west or even been reintroduced into the hills. The implications of this are twofold. Firstly, where the ground was good for farming there was every incentive to clear it of trees, so that they tend to have been left only on the poorer land. This would be, for example, on the steeper slopes or sandy heaths and also on occasional outcrops of clay, leaving just a small copse of trees on a hilltop or valley floor. Secondly, trees grow well in areas of higher rainfall, so that it was more logical to pursue forestry in, say, Devon than along the east coast. A combination of these factors was in fact part of the rationale in the twentieth century of creating new coniferous forests on the uplands of Scotland and Wales.

There is another unique feature of the British countryside that is due in part to our geographic situation, namely the patchwork of hedgerows that are almost non-existent elsewhere in Europe. It is largely because Britain is an island that we escaped being overrun by Napoleon's armies and so retained a legal system based on Roman law rather than having to adopt the Napoleonic Code as occurred throughout much of continental Europe. Under the latter, property tends on death to be divided in equal parts among all of the owner's successors with the result that farms were progressively fragmented into relatively small units. These reduced areas were held as strips or parcels of land within larger open fields, generally without any physical demarcation between them. In Britain, on the other hand, the convention has been for such property to be left in its entirety to the eldest son so that farms and estates were kept intact. There was little need then to break up existing fields or change boundaries and the hedgerows that divided them therefore remained in place. This feature of the landscape was further enhanced with the implementation of the Parliamentary Enclosure Acts, as mentioned in Chapter 7.

The countryside continues of course to adapt to changing circumstances. Land that would have been reckoned by all conventional counts to be well suited to arable cultivation has had to be left fallow in setaside. Elsewhere, some ground may be planted with new trees that have no foreseeable commercial potential. Frequently too, farm land and buildings are being converted to new uses, whether for commercial, residential or leisure purposes. As a result, the growing needs of a community that go beyond just the provision of food are being met. High-tech offices now occupy buildings that previously would have stored a precious harvest of corn, while ramblers stroll along the old drove roads that were once the means of bringing fresh meat to the towns. But amongst this tide of change and the increasing numbers of people and activities that it has brought into the countryside, there remain the essential businesses of farming and forestry. These are indeed still the mainstay of the landscape; the way in which they have evolved over the years and are now being carried out is explored in the following chapters, looking firstly at each of the separate categories of arable, pasture and upland by which the country can be broadly defined.

2 ARABLE LAND

The Seasons

The arable year begins immediately after harvest in the early autumn when the land is sown with those crops that are to be over-wintered in the ground. The most common of these are wheat, barley, oilseed rape and beans, and also in some areas linseed or oats. The residue of the previous crop, generally in the form of stubble, may be ploughed over and the soil prepared for sowing through a process of discing or harrowing and rolling. The seed itself is 'drilled' by machine which sets it just beneath the surface in rows, thus creating a distinctive characteristic of lines firstly on the surface of the ground and then in the rows of the young plants as they germinate and develop. This provides a simple way of distinguishing whether a field contains a young cereal crop or a newly sown pasture, as the two can look very similar, except that grass seed tends to be 'broadcast' or scattered and does not therefore show up in lines.

Not all crops are autumn sown and some land does therefore remain bare throughout the winter. This will be because certain crops are not suited to over-wintering and also in order to spread the workload on the farm so that not all the cultivations and the ensuing harvest need be done at the same time. Sugar beet and forage maize come into the former category as they

can only be sown in the spring, whereas the latter group includes spring varieties of most of the main winter crops mentioned. Spring cropping is a more viable alternative on lighter soils and has the advantage of requiring a lesser expenditure on treatment, although it does then tend to produce lighter yields. In some cases, the stubble may have been left until the spring in order to provide a habitat or 'cover' for game birds such as pheasant and partridge, or for 'setaside'.

The question of timing is also a factor in determining the choice of crops and the sequence in which they are grown. In order to be able to establish an autumn-sown cereal before the onset of winter, the ground will need to have been cleared of the previous harvest early in the season. A winter variety can therefore only follow a type of crop that will ripen soon enough to allow the succeeding one to be established in time. The timing of the harvest itself is dependent largely on the weather, not only at around the actual moment when the crop is fully ripened but also to some extent throughout the whole growing season, as this will have affected the development of the plants. The harvest begins in southern England in about the middle or end of July, with winter barley and oilseed rape followed by winter wheat and then the autumn-sown crops and field beans. It tends to start progressively later the further north one goes. As to when it ends, this is again determined by the weather and can be either early August or right up to October under dire conditions in Aberdeenshire!

The different seasons all impact upon the final success of the crop. For example, a wet autumn may delay the harvest and mean that the next crop is sown later than normal or into a poor seedbed, so that it is badly established and less likely to produce a good result in the following year. Most winter cereals should be sown or 'drilled' before mid-October, while oilseed rape needs to be in the ground by mid-September. Linseed and the spring cereals tend to be planted between mid-March and mid-April.

2 ARABLE LAND

The Crops

The choice of what crop is to be grown each year is determined by various factors, such as the type of soil, the situation of the farm, the principles of rotation, and also the state of the prevailing market. The crops themselves can be considered within a number of basic categories.

Combineable Crops

These, as the name implies, are crops that can be gathered in by means of a combine harvester and are grown for grain or seed, comprising essentially cereals and oil seeds.

Cereals

Ripening barley

The most common cereals in Britain are wheat and barley and, to a lesser extent, oats. Wheat is identifiable in the earlier stages of growth by its darker green foliage and then later by the full and erect appearance of the ears. It is grown for two main purposes according to variety and circumstance: either for cattle feed or for milling into flour for bread and biscuits. Barley is a lighter green when young and produces an ear that is sheathed in whiskers and tends to hang downwards. Its use, again according to circumstance, is either for cattle feed or for malting. Oats are identifiable by the fact that the ears are lighter and more open than wheat or barley. They are grown principally for horse feed and also for baking and breakfast cereal mixes. Other less common types of cereals include durum wheat, which produces semolina flour for pasta, and triticale which is a hybrid between rye and durum wheat and is processed for cattle feed. Rye is grown only rarely in Britain where there is less demand for its flour than in some other European countries, although unlike most other cereals it is well suited to light soils. Grain maize, or sweet corn, is viable only in southern England and is therefore mostly imported. The maize that can be seen growing around the country is generally cultivated as a forage crop and occasionally in small areas for shooting cover.

2 ARABLE LAND

Oilseed Rape

The dazzling yellow of rape flower has become a distinctive feature of the British landscape in early summer. Prior to this the plants are dark green in appearance, not unlike a young cabbage or the leaf of swede or turnip, to which rape is connected by being in the same family of brassicas. Indeed, the rather strange-sounding name of rape is apparently derived from the Greek (*rapys*) for turnip. Whilst in flower, it also has a particularly heady scent of pollen that somehow matches the vibrant colour. Later, the crop becomes almost ungainly, with a long stalk supporting a mass of small pods and turning a rather faded rusty colour. Rape is a rich source of vegetable oil and provides also an ingredient for cattle feed. It is a useful break crop for cereals as it allows the land to be cleaned of weed and disease and yet uses much the same machinery. Its popularity in recent years has also been encouraged by the level of guaranteed subsidies from the European Commission (EC), although latterly these have been reduced. Oilseed rape oil can furthermore be used for industrial purposes rather than for food production and as such is permitted on land that has been 'setaside'.

Linseed

Another more recent invasion of colour into the British countryside has been the blue haze of the linseed flower. Linseed is crushed to produce a non-edible oil leaving a residue that can be used in cattle feed. Like oilseed rape, its development has been encouraged by European subsidies and it also provides a good break in a cereal rotation, although it tends to be more difficult to grow and is therefore less widespread than rape. Linseed is a more delicate-looking plant than rape, growing in a more compact manner and fruiting into clusters of small seeds.

Legumes

Field beans, which look much like garden broad beans, have traditionally been a favoured break crop within a cereal rotation, but in recent years have been superseded to some extent by oilseeds. As the subsidy on the latter is reduced, one can see a return to beans which have an added

2 ARABLE LAND

Linseed

advantage of fixing nitrogen in the soil. They are used exclusively for animal feed and are harvested 'dry' when the plants seem quite withered and the pods have even blackened. Field peas, again looking not unlike the garden variety, are another combineable break crop that fit in well with cereals, allowing for weed and disease control and reintroducing some nitrogen to the soil. Although used for human consumption, they are suitable only for drying rather than for freezing. Peas for the frozen food market are obtained from vining peas which cannot be picked through a combine harvester.

One may occasionally see a field of lupins which, although slightly smaller and more dull in colour than garden varieties, do still have a striking appearance. The pods provide a high protein animal feed. Another legume that might be noticed for its small pea-like flower is lucerne or alfalfa which is grown for forage and is mentioned in Chapter 3.

2 ARABLE LAND

Root Crops

The two main types of root crops are potatoes and sugar beet, both of which need to be grown on a lighter land that allows for the crop to be harvested without undue damage or difficulty, as might be encountered on heavier land. They are therefore found in limited areas of Britain, such as the eastern counties and East Scotland, although early varieties are grown in the south west of England and Wales as well as on the Channel Islands where there is a milder climate.

Harvesting sugar beet

Sugar beet needs to be transported to processing factories and this tends also to limit the regions in which it is grown. The crop, which is spring sown, grows rapidly with a large spinach-like leaf which is sometimes cut just prior to harvest and used for cattle feed. The roots themselves when lifted can be seen stored in the open on concrete pads before being delivered to the factory. The sugar that is refined from home-grown beet is marketed under the Silver Spoon label, alongside a very similar product such as demerara sugar, which is derived from sugar cane produced in the tropics. Potatoes, which are again familiar to gardeners, with untidy green foliage above the ground and white or pale purple flowers, are planted in the spring within distinctive ridges. Root crops are grown necessarily in lighter land as they cannot be harvested as readily out of heavier land, especially now when such work is done by machine rather than by hand. Since the lighter land tends to dry out more quickly than the heavier soils, it can benefit from irrigation, which may well be seen in action over such fields. Root crops provide a useful break within a cereal rotation, as mentioned later in this chapter.

There are occasions too when fields of mangolds, swedes or turnips may still be seen. These are grown mostly as fodder for sheep when they are brought onto arable land for extra grazing and for the fertility that the flock brings to the soil.

2 ARABLE LAND

Field Vegetables

Whilst vegetables can be grown with reasonable success in almost every type of garden or allotment, on a field scale most of them require a high-quality, free-draining soil that can be cultivated over a longer season than a heavier and wetter ground. This allows for mechanisation and for an early crop to be produced at the required high standards. Commercial vegetable production is therefore concentrated on certain areas such as East Kent, the eastern counties, the Chichester Plain and the Vale of Evesham. As a consequence, the processing plants tend to be located in the same areas and, as the speed at which a crop is transferred from the field to the processing plant is generally crucial, there is a further concentration of production in these particular districts. As with root crops, these high-quality soils are of a light structure and can be liable to dry out so that irrigation may well be used in the summer.

Some field vegetables such as brassicas thrive on heavier soils and this explains, for example, the tradition for growing brussel sprouts and cabbages on the clay land of Bedfordshire. Peas are also grown on a variety of soils; whether for drying or vining, as mentioned above. The vining peas that are prepared for the frozen food market have to be grown in specific areas that are not far from the processing plants. This is because in order to freeze peas successfully it is essential that the minimum of time is lost between harvesting and processing. The harvest itself involves the use of specialised machinery known as pea viners that would dwarf many ordinary combine harvesters and are often worked around the clock. Other field-scale vegetables that can be seen in the more intensive arable areas include leeks and dwarf beans which can both be cultivated mechanically and, on a smaller scale, runner beans which require staking and hand picking. Pick Your Own ventures are able to produce a further range of intensive crops such as courgettes.

Successful vegetable cropping depends not only on having the right soils but also on securing the right markets. Quality and timing can be crucial in

2 ARABLE LAND

selling a crop to its best advantage. Even in an era when so many 'fresh' foods are imported from around the world, there tends to be a premium for the first produce from the local season. This explains why early potatoes are grown in some south-westerly regions of the country that are otherwise given over more to grassland and why one may see fields in eastern England being covered in springtime by vast sheets of plastic or

artificial fleece. The plastic sheets have an essential purpose of warming the soil below and thereby speeding up the development of crops such as carrots, as well as of suppressing competitive weed growth and reducing insect damage. The newer alternative use of fleece also helps to retain moisture around the roots of the crop which is grown on earth ridges between the fleece.

Fruit

Fruit in a farming context is defined by two basic categories: top fruit and soft fruit.

Top fruit describes those that grow on trees, such as apples and pears, although many of the modern varieties are on dwarf stocks that are smaller than the traditional orchards and easier therefore to maintain and harvest. The market for home-grown apples and pears has been much affected by the increasing availability of imports, especially from the southern hemisphere at times of the year when the local produce will have had to have been kept in cold storage. There has also been a change in demand as consumers become accustomed to new varieties of fruit and to the high quality with which they tend to be offered. For example, a former mainstay of the British market, the Cox's Orange Pippin, could retain its best condition in storage for only a few months and would be prone to slight markings on the skin. Meanwhile, some imported varieties have become available in seemingly perfect order. There are still occasionally signs of old cherry orchards in southern England, but most have now also succumbed to the high cost of labour for hand picking and the competition from supplies from Mediterranean countries that have an earlier and more reliable climate. Plums continue to be grown in certain areas, notably around Pershore and Evesham in Hereford and Worcester, and are an example of what is termed stone fruit. Commercial top fruit growing is now mostly confined to a few localities in England, such as Kent and the West Midlands. Cider apples are still being grown in the areas around Somerset and Herefordshire. A major hazard for these crops is late frost which can kill the blossom before it has 'set' into fruit and orchards tend therefore to be found in protected, southerly positions.

Soft fruit refers to those that grow on canes or bushes, such as raspberries or blackcurrants, or on the ground, such as strawberries. Late frosts can also be a problem for these crops, although some do also benefit from long summer daylight and therefore thrive in northerly areas like eastern Scotland. The more popular soft fruits are often a significant part of Pick Your Own ventures, but many are grown for wholesale and for processing into, for example, fruit juice. Some of these, such as blackcurrants, can be harvested mechanically and may be protected from frosts by irrigation, giving rise occasionally to the otherwise illogical sight of a crop being watered on a cold spring morning.

2 ARABLE LAND

Hop harvest

Hop gardens used to be a familiar feature of Kent and parts of the West Midlands, but are now more rare as an increasing share of the trade is imported from the Continent. These 'gardens' are very distinctive as the hops are trained up high wires strung between tall poles, although the more modern varieties are again of a more compact nature. The harvested hops have to be dried before being used in brewing and this used to be done in oast houses that are still widely seen throughout the Kent and Sussex landscape. These have, however, now all been converted to residential use and hops are dried in modern kilns that are less eye-catching and far less numerous.

Vineyards have been re-introduced into England (vines having been grown here originally in Roman times), but with one exception these tend to be only a few acres in extent. The rows of vines themselves are not therefore readily noticed within the landscape, although the signboards advertising the sale of wine may serve as evidence of this local industry. Whilst vineyards in continental Europe are also in small individual ownerships, the distinctive patchwork effect of lines of vines that can be seen in France and Germany is rarely repeated in Britain, as they are rather few and far between and often enclosed by hedgerows. In the southern half of the country, vines of certain selected varieties are able to produce a harvest of grapes suitable for wine making. This is mostly white wine based on the Müller-Thurgau grape although a number of other varieties are now also grown, including a few red wines. Dessert grapes require a more sunny climate and are not grown commercially in Britain.

Horticulture

In this context, horticulture refers to those crops that are grown under cover, usually in large banks of glasshouses or in polythene tunnels. These are generally either for the intensive production of salad crops or for ornamental plants and flowers and tend to be concentrated in specific areas according to the particular benefits that those locations might offer. One

14

2 ARABLE LAND

prerequisite is having the right quality of soil that is capable of being cultivated intensively and versatile enough to support a variety of horticultural crops. This points to the areas of Grade 1 land referred to in Chapter 11 and which are found in the fens of the eastern counties and in areas of Lancashire, Hereford and Worcestershire and parts of southern England. Another factor is that of climate and length of natural light, as there is a crucial market advantage in being able to produce such crops earlier than one's competitors and with lower heating costs. This explains the concentration of glasshouse developments in some areas on the southern edge of the country where temperatures may be milder than elsewhere and where summer days are longer, such as around Chichester or in Cornwall or on the Isle of Wight. It would not, however, apply so well to other regions where one can see glasshouses and polytunnels, notably to the north of Liverpool or around Evesham or along the Lea Valley in Hertfordshire. In these cases, another, rather historic, factor provides the reason, namely the need to be near to large areas of urban populations in the days when it was difficult to transport fresh produce over long distances. As opposed to field-scale vegetables that are often best grown close to processing plants, as mentioned above, salad crops are frequently prepared and packaged on the farms where they are cultivated. Some glasshouses, such as in Humberside, are sited near to power stations and other industrial units from which they are able to gain a direct supply of heat and power.

In the present day, transport represents a growing element of cost but need no longer affect the condition of the foodstuffs that are being carried. Indeed, nowadays English growers face great competition from all manner of fresh foods and flowers that are flown in from overseas or brought in by refrigerated lorries from southern Europe. Even with the cost of transportation, these imports are being sold at no more and often less than home-grown produce. This is partly due to seasonal differences, in that in equatorial Africa or in the southern hemisphere such crops can be readily harvested at a time when Britain is struggling with winter. Even in the

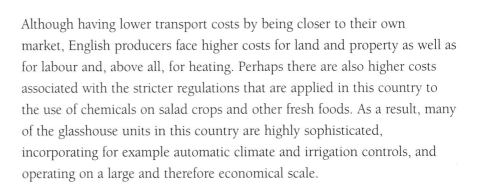

south of Spain the cropping season is much longer than in England, extending over most of the year, and some British growers have had to seize the advantage that this gives by setting up their own production units over there.

Although having lower transport costs by being closer to their own market, English producers face higher costs for land and property as well as for labour and, above all, for heating. Perhaps there are also higher costs associated with the stricter regulations that are applied in this country to the use of chemicals on salad crops and other fresh foods. As a result, many of the glasshouse units in this country are highly sophisticated, incorporating for example automatic climate and irrigation controls, and operating on a large and therefore economical scale.

The main crops grown in this way are lettuces, tomatoes and cucumbers, together with a growing output of a wide range of pot plants for garden centres and other outlets. Another intensive horticultural crop that is widely grown under cover is mushrooms. However, as these thrive with only limited light, the buildings are either enclosed timber sheds or darkened polytunnels. The mushrooms are grown generally on a special compost and not in ordinary soil.

Some glasshouses may have no soil inside them and incorporate instead a hydroponic system in which the plants are grown entirely in water into which is added a necessary mix of nutrients. Tomatoes, peppers and cucumbers are the main crops that can be grown by this system which allows for greater flexibility but demands a very precise standard of management.

Industrial and Non-Food Crops
Arable farmland is now sometimes being used to grow crops that are destined for industrial use rather than food production. This is still on a limited scale and therefore not widely seen around the country. European grant aid that was introduced to encourage flax and hemp to be cultivated

2 ARABLE LAND

for fibre production has now been reduced. Oilseed rape and linseed are also being grown for conversion into industrial oils and this is even a permissible use of land under setaside. In certain parts of the country, willow and poplar saplings can be seen growing in fields for harvesting for fuel, as well as the less familiar miscanthus or elephant grass. This 'biomass', as it is known, is used primarily for generating electricity in specially constructed power stations and, since it is relatively bulky and therefore expensive to transport, it tends still to be in only very restricted areas close to where such facilities have been developed.

Small areas of herbs and other crops are being grown for the pharmaceutical industry, some of which are particularly colourful and therefore noticeable, such as borage or evening primrose. Daffodils and to a lesser extent tulips can be seen growing on a field scale. These tend to be on lighter soils and may be either for picking as blooms, in which case they will be in a location such as Cornwall that benefits from a mild climate and therefore an early season, or to sell as bulbs.

Game Crops

Although the arable landscape tends now to comprise large fields of uniform crops, there are occasions when one may see small strips where something different is being grown. These strips are likely to be left standing throughout the winter or be planted alongside a hedge line or shelter belt of trees. Such plantings, or 'game crops', are created for the benefit of the shoot, in that they provide cover and feed for pheasants and other game birds. They tend therefore to be in strategic areas for shooting purposes, whether as an extension to a natural feature such as a shelter belt or to encourage the birds to collect in what would otherwise be open ground. Typical game crops are maize, kale and root artichoke, which all grow to a good height and are able to over-winter.

Crop Varieties

For most of us it is enough just to be able to identify the particular type of

2 ARABLE LAND

crop being grown, but farmers and processors have to be involved with a wide range of different varieties. One basic distinction comes from the use to which the crop will be put: wheat may be either for milling (into flour for bread and biscuits) or for animal feed; barley can be for feed or for malting (in breweries or whisky distilleries); and some potatoes are selected for a particular purpose whether for baking or for processing into chips or crisps. Within these essential categories there are an enormous number of specific varieties, each of which will have particular characteristics relating to the way that they grow and also their end use. These will include considerations of reliability, suitability to certain localities, disease resistance and yield, as well as popularity with buyers.

Therefore once a farmer has decided on what type of crops to grow and in what system of rotation, he will still have to determine which variety of those crops would be the most appropriate. They often carry exotic sounding names, such as Malacca (wheat), Regina (barley), Stallion (sugar beet) and Desirée (potatoes), which are just occasionally posted up on the roadside edge of a field as an advertisement for the supplier. Varieties of the same crop all look much the same to the inexpert eye, although some do have more obvious features such as wheat with a short straw or potatoes with a purple rather than white flower. In general, milling wheat and malting barley need to be grown to more exacting standards than feed crops and therefore require good conditions in terms of soil and climate as well as a more intensive, and more expensive, management. They tend to produce slightly lighter yields per hectare, but attract a premium price of perhaps 20% or so over the more basic feed varieties.

Plant Breeding
Most crop varieties will have been developed through cross-breeding different strains using the results of a continual programme of research that has been going on around the world for decades and even centuries. The concept of genetically modifying crops is an extension of this botanical process, but introduces genetic material from other species in order to

provide a desired characteristic such as resistance to disease. The introduction of genetically modified crops to the British countryside has evoked much discussion and controversy about what the consequences might be, not only to the consumer but also to the countryside. This might create an image of alien-looking crops, but in fact when growing in the field these genetically modified organisms (GMOs) will look no different to any other crop.

Evidence of scientific work being done on arable crops can sometimes be seen in the form of trial plots. Parts of a field are marked out with sticks forming strips or rectangular areas within which the crop will have been sown with particular varieties or treated in different ways. On occasions there will be very visible variations between these plots, where some may have failed or seemingly outgrown the others, but generally the results will be discernible only through scientific assessment.

Setaside

Since 1992, the Common Agricultural Policy (CAP) has been able to provide some control over the total volume of food production by a requirement that farmers leave some land unplanted each year. This policy applies to all but the smaller farms and is a condition that needs to be observed if the business is to qualify for Arable Aid Payments. The proportion of land that has to be setaside in this manner can be varied by the EC according to circumstances and has ranged from 5% to 15%. Currently at 10%, its effects can be seen around the country as certain fields appear rather ragged and uneven in appearance with a mixture of weeds and regenerated crops. Some management is permitted in order to prepare for the following season or to control the growth on the land, including the use of certain herbicides, but this is generally restricted in the spring and early summer so as to encourage wildlife habitats and other conservation features. Cultivations for the following season are permitted after July 15 and this is the reason that land can be seen being ploughed in mid-July before any of that year's harvest has taken place. The previously setaside fields will still only be sown at the most suitable time in the autumn, but the 'early entry' for ploughing and other cultivations will have helped spread the work load in the post-harvest period.

Setaside may give the land an untidy and almost derelict look, but it does provide a good habitat for wildlife, especially for songbirds. It is normally rotational and incorporated within the overall cropping system on the farm, although there are occasions when it can be retained permanently on one particular area. This policy is often ridiculed as paying farmers to do nothing, but it is more accurately a case of being paid compensation for not being allowed to grow food on one tenth of the farm in any one year. The land does still need to be maintained even when left uncultivated and may indeed sometimes be used for non-food crops as mentioned above.

Practice

The succession of crops is also determined largely by the practice of rotation. Although it is often assumed that modern arable farming is given over to a uniformity of intensive cropping that is artificially sustained by chemicals, it does in fact still adhere to the traditional concept of rotation whereby growing crops of the same type in close succession is avoided. This helps to maintain fertility and reduce disease and means that each field will tend to support a different crop from year to year. Where one may have seen, for example, the yellow flowers of oilseed rape last summer, one is likely in the following year to find another vista of perhaps the dark green of wheat. Some crops, such as cereals, could be grown on the same land year after year, provided that they are intensively treated with fertiliser and other chemicals, but others, especially root crops such as potatoes, sugar beet or carrots, are likely to suffer infestations against which there is no viable protection and which would remain in the soil for several seasons.

2 ARABLE LAND

Adopting a conventional rotation cannot alone ensure protection against losses in yields, whether through diminished fertility or from fungal damage or attack by insects. To maintain the level and quality of production demanded by today's markets, it is generally considered necessary to apply either nutrients or controlling agents such as pesticides or weedkillers. These tend now to be used as efficiently as possible and only when circumstances demand, such as when there are signs of aphids on the crop or when the temperature makes it particularly responsive to fertiliser. To achieve this, the farmer needs to be able to take tractors with sprayers onto the land at specific times and without then damaging the growing crop. This is facilitated by leaving narrow tracks of bare land at intervals within the drilled lines of the crop and along which the tractor wheels can then be driven. The distance between these wheel marks or 'tramlines' is determined by the width of the spraying booms so that the entire field can be covered by working up and down each track. As an alternative, a field of crops might be sprayed from an aeroplane or helicopter, although this is now relatively rare due to the considerably greater cost.

2 ARABLE LAND

Where organic crops are being grown, there is no requirement for applying such artificial ingredients and no call therefore to create tramlines. Yields tend to be lower than when using more conventional systems, with a more selective use of fertiliser and with weeds and pests then being controlled by other means. The casual observer may therefore see little difference between a well-managed organic crop and one that is being grown conventionally, other than in the absence of tramlines. Cereal crops may perhaps appear to be taller and less dense and if there are weeds they are likely to appear right across the crop rather than in isolated pockets. On occasions when a field is infested by weed, such as the eye-catching red of poppies, it is more likely to mean that the farmer has failed to apply the necessary herbicide than that it is necessarily within an organic system. Sometimes, it may be just a band of weed across one part of a field and this would suggest that there had been a temporary failure in application, such as the spray nozzles becoming blocked or the tank running dry. Embarrassing as this may be for the tractor driver, it does give an indication of how widespread such weeds could be if they were not treated and also of how effective the herbicides are.

Generally, however, arable crops within the British landscape are remarkably consistent and seemingly clear of weeds. The lack of weeds is due largely to the availability of modern herbicides and to increasingly sophisticated management techniques. That these techniques are so assiduously applied is a function of the fact that for so long the emphasis in farming in Britain was to increase production and to achieve high standards of quality. Under such conditions, the agrochemical industry was able to develop increasingly effective ingredients at an economic price. These ingredients could be utilised by farmers who then gained premium returns from the resulting higher quality crops and heavier yields. In more recent times there has been a growing emphasis on being more selective in the use of chemicals, for both environmental and economic reasons. However, the requirement for high-quality produce still remains and if a crop is allowed to have within it traces of weed or other impurities, it will

2 ARABLE LAND

be more difficult to sell and likely to achieve only a reduced price. Farmers
continue therefore to be committed to producing clean and consistent
crops and their fields will continue to reflect this sometimes sanitised
standard of management.

The sight of a sprayer working methodically through a field and seemingly
drenching it with chemicals may be rather unappealing and even quite
sinister. In fact what is being applied will be greatly diluted with water and
will furthermore be a compound that has been subjected to extremely
stringent tests. These sprays have three essential functions: herbicides to
kill weeds; insecticides to control damage by insects such as aphids; and
fungicides to reduce the incidence of various forms of mould and disease.
Another common application, although usually broadcast in pellet form, is
of molluscicides to counter damage by slugs. These are all basically the
same materials that can be seen displayed in great profusion in any garden
centre. The agri-chemicals are rather more sophisticated versions that tend
to be quite costly and the way in which they are used is therefore quite
sophisticated too. The condition of the crops and the soil, as well as the
prevailing state of the weather, is carefully monitored and chemical
remedies are only applied when there is a good case to do so. It would be
unprofitable and unproductive to use sprays like a sort of blanket insurance
policy against all possible ills. As the use of these products has become so
sophisticated, many farmers use agronomists, or crop walkers, to advise
them on the condition of their fields and the best possible remedies. These
crop walkers may be seen, as their name implies, going through the fields
where they will be looking for crucial signs of such things as tiny black
aphids or brown blotches on leaves.

Another instance of people walking through crops (other than trespassers!)
highlights the importance of eliminating impurities and the fact that
chemical sprays may be either too limited in effect or too costly. In this case
they would have bags on their backs into which they appear to be putting
some of the cereal plants that they have just pulled out of the ground by

Wheat damaged by slugs

23

hand. This is not vandalism but 'hand roguing' wild oats, which is a weed that can spread through cereal crops and can be difficult to eradicate being botanically so similar to, for example, wheat or barley. Wild oats are very similar in appearance to the cultivated variety, with a spread and feathery seed head, but are taller than the other cereals and can therefore be seen rising up above the main crop. Hand weeding on a field scale can also sometimes be seen on land that is being farmed organically.

Wild oats can also be chemically treated if necessary and are no longer as widespread as in the past. Other common weeds in cereal crops that tend to stand out are grasses such as couch, blackgrass and sterile brome which spreads particularly around the headlands. Especially visible and occasionally very virulent, although normally not difficult to control, is the poppy, with its dashing red colour.

The herbicides that are used in arable farming are mostly all of a selective nature so that they suppress only certain weeds and leave the cultivated crop looking lush and rather uniform. The only indication therefore that they have been applied is in the fact that there is little or no sign of any of the other, unwanted, plants. Sometimes, however, a whole field appears to have been killed off and turned a dried brown colour. This is likely to be after a period of setaside or when grassland is about to be ploughed over for arable cultivation and when all the weeds and grasses have been sprayed off to reduce their re-emergence within the new crop. Whilst this may have a rather drastic appearance, almost like a scorched earth policy, it will in fact be done by the use of a straightforward glyphosate product such as that sold in garden centres for clearing paths or borders of weeds. Occasionally still, this treatment may be seen being applied along the margins of the field (the 'headlands'), with the purpose of creating a barrier to prevent weeds from spreading from the bank or hedgerow into the field itself.

The fertiliser spreader may evoke a similar response to the sight of a sprayer at work, especially as the granules being broadcast across the land

2 ARABLE LAND

will be described as 'artificial' fertiliser. This provides three essential ingredients that most arable crops depend upon and therefore take from the soil as they grow: namely nitrogen, potassium and phosphorous. If these are not replaced, the successive crops will fail to flourish and become prone to disease. Retaining or replacing nitrogen can be achieved in part by rotation and by animal manuring as mentioned previously, but in most commercial arable enterprises it will have to be provided or at least supplemented by artificial means. This comprises a basic chemical compound such as ammonium nitrate or urea for the nitrogen and, for example, superphosphate and sulphate of potash, all of which are naturally absorbed in the soil and taken up by the crops. Increasing attention is being paid to the 'leaching' of nitrates when some of what has been applied may be washed through the soil before being absorbed by the plant roots, and then enter the natural watercourses. In areas where land types are particularly vulnerable to leaching, the fertiliser will be spread only at times when the crops have developed sufficiently to respond to the available nitrogen. As with sprays, artificial fertilisers have become increasingly expensive and are therefore being used more sparingly, even to the extent of analysing different soils in different parts of fields and reducing the application where it is needed least. One technique for achieving this even uses satellite mapping linked directly to the tractor cab as it passes over the relevant parts of a field.

Lime spreading

In some areas, a spreader may be seen at work seemingly dusting the land with a coating of white. This is in fact what it appears to be, namely chalk or some other natural form of lime. Plants not only need the right nutrients and degree of moisture but also are sensitive to the acidity of the soil. Where this tends to be high it becomes necessary to reduce it to an acceptable level by applying an alkaline material such as lime. This is then retained in the soil for some years and so is a less frequent operation than spreading fertiliser.

2 ARABLE LAND

Since the chemicals that are used in farming are now so sophisticated and selective, it is difficult to know what is actually being applied to the land whenever a sprayer is at work in the fields. There are, however, some general methods that might be observed: if it is before the new crop has appeared in the ground, then it is likely that a herbicide is being applied; if the crop is newly established, then it could be either a 'top dressing' of fertiliser or an aphicide, although these are now being more sparingly used; in either of these early stages a slug treatment might also be made; once the crop is in a more lush state of growth, it would be fungicides that are needed and possibly a late application of liquid nitrogen on a winter-sown crop.

Spraying oilseed rape in flower

Organic farming is discussed in Chapter 11, but in the present context it might be asked why the use of chemical sprays and artificial fertilisers is so commonplace, given that they are so expensive and unappealing, and why the alternative of an organic method is not more widely used instead. The brief answer to this is, firstly, that organic farming generally produces lower yields whilst requiring a more intensive, and thus more expensive, system of management. Even with the cost saving of not having to buy and apply chemicals, it still depends upon being able to achieve higher prices in order to be viable. There is a limit, however, to the number of consumers who are sufficiently concerned about the nature of their food to pay such a premium for it. Some retailers may subsidise the price of organic goods as a marketing exercise, but there is otherwise no regular support for producers except during the period of conversion from conventional farming. This conversion process can take a number of years before the land can be considered to be clear of any residue of artificial ingredients that may have been applied previously. On a day-to-day basis therefore, the market would not at present sustain more than a limited amount of organic production.

Taking a wider view, there are questions also as to how the necessary levels of fertility and minerals could be maintained if organic systems were to be the sole method of food production in the developed world. It is anyway extremely difficult for an all-arable farm to be totally organic when it has no source of animal manure with which to boost fertility. Of course, a livestock venture could be introduced onto the farm, although this might then take up land that should really be better used for arable cropping. An alternative

Sheep within an arable system

2 ARABLE LAND

is to rely on a relatively intensive form of livestock such as pigs or poultry that take up less land than, for example, sheep or cattle. These are, however, quite specialised and capital intensive and not therefore always feasible, as well as being incompatible with organic principles. Also, arable organic farming is not easily adapted to all soil types, due to the greater emphasis on cultivations and the need therefore to be able to go on to the land more frequently but without damaging either the crop or the land. Another restricting factor is the need to avoid areas where there is more likelihood of infestations such as from slugs, which are less easy to control by organic methods than with chemical molluscicides.

Lodged barley

Even within modern conventional farming there can be two particular occasions when the land does not appear to be kept in immaculate commercial order. One such instance is setaside, whereby fields are left uncultivated under a policy that is outlined in Chapter 9. Its effect on the landscape is, however, to create an eye-catching contrast to the manicured arable fields that surround it. Another very visible interruption to the consistency of a crop can occur when sections of it appear to be blown down. Less regular and certainly more rational than crop circles, this 'lodging' results from gusts of wind or heavy downpours of rain. There may be occasions when the weather conditions are such that this damage cannot be avoided, but it can also arise as a direct consequence of the management of the crop, when for example the amount of fertiliser applied produces a weight of grain that was too great for the strength of the straw upon which it was grown. An indication of how farming has developed in recent times is seen in the fact that to reduce the risk of lodging the farmer does not necessarily cut back on the use of fertiliser and accept a lesser yield, but applies instead a 'growth regulator' that restricts the length of the straw and hence reduces its vulnerability to violent weather. Eddies of wind coming off hedgerows and an uneven growth in the crop are other possible causes of lodging. Crop circles and other such patterns that have been swathed neatly through growing corn are seen more frequently in the media than actually on the ground. Their origin and purpose is never fully explained and remains seemingly a mystery, although they are certainly not part of a farming process!

There is a growing tendency also to leave the margins of the field, or headlands, to grow wild. This practice is even supported to a degree under the aid payment system and is intended to provide a strip of natural habitat for wildlife. Previously, such headlands might have been ploughed up and sprayed with herbicide in order to create a sterile strip and prevent the hedgerow weeds from spreading into the crop itself. More normally, the crop would be grown right up to edge of the field, even though the outermost plants might not thrive as well as elsewhere. This would be due to competition from the hedge, which takes moisture from the roots and creates shade, as well as to the extra compaction of the soil resulting from tractors and implements being turned round. In some areas, the planted headlands may have been eaten down by rabbits, deer or pheasants whose grazing tends to be concentrated on the outer edges of a field. This means that yields from the headland areas are anyway reduced, and so leaving them under grass or other natural foliage causes only a limited loss to the crop as a whole. There has been some controversy within the European Commission recently regarding the acceptable width of hedgerows. It was suggested that if farmers allowed their hedges to grow out to more than 2 metres they would forego part of their arable aid payments, but this proposed regulation has now been withdrawn.

Many types of farmland, other than the lighter or more stony soils, need drainage. This is largely hidden from view, being constructed underground as explained in the later section on subsoiling. Field boundaries often incorporate a ditch for the purpose of draining away any surplus water. This process is important, particularly in heavier soils, as it allows the ground to be cultivated more readily and helps prevent the roots of the crop becoming waterlogged. Drained land is also less cold and crops will grow more rapidly when the soil is able to dry out and warm up. A network of underground pipes or 'mole' drains needs to be replaced every

2 ARABLE LAND

few years, with the actual frequency depending on the type of soil. They usually run into open ditches which have to be kept clear of silt and weed and are therefore dug out on a more regular basis. The outfalls of the underdrains can be seen in the banks of these ditches and may often be running with water some while after a period of rainfall. Drainage work tends to be done in the winter when the land is bare of crops.

Monoculture

Traditionally, the growing of arable crops would often have been integrated with a livestock enterprise. This would have had two main functions: firstly, supplying the local community with basic, and perishable, foodstuffs; and secondly, providing essential fertility to the arable land through farmyard manure. The synergy would have been continued furthermore in that where livestock was housed in barns or yards in the winter it would have been bedded on straw. This would have not only provided a useful constituent for the farmyard manure but also utilised what might otherwise be a waste product from the cereal crops.

That such mixed farming has now become less common has several ramifications for present-day agriculture, as outlined below, but it is interesting too to note the signs that are still visible within the countryside of these earlier systems.

Hedgerows, which may have provided physical evidence of legal occupations, were essentially a physical means of containing livestock on their pastures and now have little purpose on arable land. In the days when the rotation incorporated grazing, such hedges would have been an essential feature on a farm and the arable cropping would have been worked within them. Before the advent of large machinery, this would have presented few problems, but as farming became more mechanised and more specialised these hedges became restrictive and superfluous. As a consequence, many were grubbed up and removed during recent times, although many do still remain even in the purely arable regions, as a

2 ARABLE LAND

vestige of how the land was farmed and occupied in a previous era. Sometimes, the hedge itself may no longer exist but its earlier presence might yet be seen in a line of old hedgerow trees that have been left standing. The subject of hedgerows is considered in a wider context in Chapter 7.

Also still visible in some arable areas are the barns that used to accommodate the livestock in the winter, often situated at some central point away from the main farmstead. In the eastern counties, these would be known as crew yards and be built of local brick or weather-boarding. In an area such as the Cotswolds these would be again of a local material, namely stone and tile.

Straw

A more current consequence of running a purely arable system is that there is no longer any requirement for straw. Sometimes it can be sold to livestock farmers who have no cereal production of their own and indeed one can often see in the autumn time lorries laden with massive bales of straw travelling from the arable areas of the east to the dairy lands in the west. This is not, however, a ready market for all, as the costs of baling and carting a relatively low-value product such as straw can make the exercise rather marginal. Furthermore, not all livestock systems still rely on straw for bedding, as mentioned in Chapter 4. In many cases therefore, the straw needs to be disposed of and until relatively recently one feature of the arable landscape in the late summer would be of huge plumes of smoke rising from the stubble fields as the straw and stubbles were simply burnt off. This is now prohibited for all but a few special crops such as linseed, and farmers have responded by finding new methods of incorporating the unwanted straw back in to the soil. In fact, the modern varieties of cereals have been bred to produce a shorter stem of straw and such crops are now much more compact than previously. Other crops have meanwhile been introduced to the landscape, such as oilseed rape, that produce a different type of straw that is more difficult to deal with than the more traditional ones of wheat and barley. The ban on the burning of straw was introduced largely for environmental and safety reasons, although burning has been in practice for many centuries as a means of cleaning and fertilising the land. One consequence arising from this ban has been an increase in slug infestation.

There have been developments in finding alternative uses for straw, such as manufacturing it into packaging material or burning it as a source of energy, although these are still limited in scope. Thatched roofs would appear to require straw when being repaired or renovated, but many of these are in fact made of reeds and those that are of straw need it to be of traditional varieties that have been specially grown, so as to produce the right length and cellular structure.

Stooks of thatching straw

Bird Scaring

The tranquility of the countryside can sometimes be shaken by the sound of what would seem to be intermittent gunfire, even outside the shooting season and particularly in the spring and early summer or autumn. The source of this will be found in automatic bird scarers which are placed within those young crops, notably oilseed rape, that are especially vulnerable to being damaged by foraging pigeons and other birds. Looking a bit like a cross between a large watering can and a mortar launching device, these scarers work by allowing a small amount of water to build up every so often and then drip onto an explosive chemical. The spout may look as if it might shoot out buckshot or worse but it is in fact only designed to project the sound rather than ammunition and is harmless, if irritating! The task is also done more peacefully by ultrasonic sound as well as by having strips of cloth or plastic staked across a field like small flags or even with cut-out models or still occasionally good old-fashioned scarecrows. Small helium balloons and dummies of owls or hawks are further examples of more peaceful versions of scarecrows.

Pigeons are sometimes controlled to some degree by shooting, often at dusk with the guns standing half hidden beneath the trees on the edge of fields. Migrating geese that literally flock over to this country in winter can cause

2 ARABLE LAND

considerable damage to young standing crops, not only by eating the plants but then also by the resultant over manuring and by the trampling effect of their large webbed feet.

Machinery and Equipment

It would be inappropriate to try within this book to give a detailed account of all the equipment used in arable farming, but it might be useful to have some description of the main items that can be seen working in the fields (or perhaps crawling ahead of a line of traffic on a country road!).

Tractors

The tractor is almost a trademark of agriculture and is indeed being used as one of the symbols for British farming produce. The trend towards larger fields and a smaller workforce has meant that tractors have also become bigger over the years. The greater power and more sophisticated mechanics of modern tractors enables them to draw larger equipment and, with fewer hedges and boundaries, to cover more ground in a working day. Not only does this provide for savings in labour costs but also it means that vital field work can be done in a shorter time, using to best advantage the moments when weather and soil conditions are most suited to the tasks in hand. Time management in farming is not just a matter of organising work shifts and overtime rates, but a constant adjustment to the weather too. The tractors may be capable of working in all conditions, especially now that most of them have the versatility of four-wheel drive and the comfort of enclosed cabs, often even with air conditioning! The work that they have to perform, however, can be of a more sensitive nature; for example, seed drilled into a wet and heavy soil will be less likely to produce a successful crop than when sown under better conditions. The tractors themselves can also damage the land that they work over, especially when it is wet. Some of these problems are reduced by modifying working practices, such as may be seen with tractors using large flotation tyres or double wheels, or

2 ARABLE LAND

working on frosty ground to avoid sinking into soft wet ground which would create ruts and reduce performance. The tyres themselves can be a sophisticated part of the tractor's equipment, costing many hundreds of pounds each and yet also be vulnerable to certain types of terrain, so that when working on stony land they will last less long than on a less abrasive surface.

The size of a tractor is a question not only of field size but also of soil types. It requires more power to pull equipment through the heavier soils than the lighter ones, so that the latter can be worked with a smaller tractor even if it is over large open areas such as those found in the fens of East Anglia. While perhaps an average tractor will be a four-wheel drive machine producing around 100 horsepower, one can also see at work massive articulated units and those with tracked drives like updated versions of military tanks. These huge modern machines may provide the economies and advantages just referred to but they do also need to be

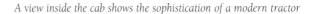

A view inside the cab shows the sophistication of a modern tractor

financed, sometimes at costs of well over £100,000 each. This may not be justifiable on even a larger individual enterprise, especially in the present climate, and it is possible that some of those seen at work will belong to contractors who operate over more than one farm and for whom the need for speed and efficiency is particularly important.

One of the most remarkable features of the modern tractor has been the development of hydraulics. This enables equipment to be lifted and controlled from the driving unit, rather than just towed along. Such attachments can be operated both from the rear, as in the case of a plough or grass cutter, and from the front of the tractor when working particularly with a fork lift or other devices. Most attachments are now run from the tractor's engine, so that a baler or forage harvester need not have its own engine but merely a facility to connect to the tractor's PTO or 'power takeoff'.

Another noticeable innovation in tractors is the gearing, which allows them to travel on roads at reasonable speeds whilst also being able to work with heavy equipment across the fields.

For those interested in the makes of vehicles, the different marques of tractors can be more easily identified than motor cars even though they are less familiar. The reason for this is that each company produces all its tractors in just one distinctive colour. A blue tractor will be a Ford New Holland, bright red Massey Ferguson or the darker red of Case, yellow Renault, green John Deere, to mention but some of the main manufacturers. A white tractor is likely to be a Lamborghini, but do not expect it to be racing around the countryside as it is constructed rather differently to the glamorous sports car of the same name!

ATVs

As tractors become bigger, there has been a growing purpose for ATVs or All-Terrain Vehicles. Looking like four-wheeled motorbikes, these can now often been seen driven across farmland as a one-man personnel carrier.

2 ARABLE LAND

Their use is, however, more common when tending livestock rather than for arable work.

Cultivations

Ploughing

The first operation in the arable season tends to be ploughing, although it may be preceded by spraying or even be superseded by discing and direct drilling. Ploughing is a familiar sight and still uses effectively the old traditional method of turning the soil into lines of furrows. What has, however, changed since the horse-drawn days is that it is now done with more than just a single ploughshare and that the plough itself may be reversible. The number of plough shares is determined by soil type and the weight and power of the tractor as mentioned above, but can be as many as nine or sometimes more. The reversible feature enables the ploughman to work the field in two directions on an immediately adjacent line rather than having, as previously, to work in a rectangle on opposite sides. This is a function again of the power of the tractor and of the ability of the hydraulics to turn the plough over at each line. This sort of plough can be recognised by the fact that it has two sets of shares, one of which appears upside down along the centre line of the equipment. The larger versions may also have a rubber-tyred wheel at the end to facilitate turning on the headlands and on which it is transported when not in use in the field, as it would not be feasible for the plough to be carried raised off the ground on the rear hydraulics of the tractor.

Seedbed Preparation

Depending on circumstances, ploughing will be followed by harrowing, discing, rolling and then drilling. The plough tends to leave a series of mounded up furrows that need to be broken down and levelled into a firm but friable seedbed. This can be done by discing which involves an implement comprising a series of vertical metal plates like smaller versions of a plough but mounted more closely together. Harrowing does a similar

2 ARABLE LAND

function either by means of a line of tines mounted behind the tractor or a flat metal mat or 'chain' of spikes that is dragged along the ground. For heavier soils, this work may be more effectively achieved by use of a power harrow, in which the tines are vibrated mechanically through a power linkage off the tractor, rather like a garden rotovator. In some cases, in order to produce a sufficiently fine seedbed the land will then also be rolled, both before and after drilling. A growing crop of autumn-sown cereal may be rolled in early spring in order to consolidate the ground after it has been loosened and lifted by frost. This then compacts the soil around the roots.

The seed drill itself runs behind a tractor and is in the form of either a conical hopper or rectangular tank. From this a series of hoses feed the seed to immediately behind a row of discs, by which means it is buried into the ground. The drill can dispense either seed alone, set to a very precise rate of application, or a combination of seed and granular fertiliser. A similar hopper may be seen mounted on the back of a tractor from which granular artificial fertiliser is broadcast over the field through a spinning dispenser.

In some cases, the process of seedbed preparation can be avoided by the use of direct drilling. This is a practice whereby the seed is sown directly into the ground into grooves made by discs that are incorporated within the seed drill. This is done into the stubble of the previous crop and without the need for ploughing. It has the economic advantage of involving fewer tractor operations, although other benefits of having the land worked over each year may be missed and it is in any case only feasible on certain types of soils.

Seed potatoes tend to be planted under ridges that will have been formed by a special type of plough and which can then be identified by the marked pattern of bare earth that remains. Potatoes tend to be grown in soils that are free from stone, as these interfere with the mechanical harvesting. In some areas a stone separator may be used to collect up the stones before ridging and then to dump them on the field edge.

2 ARABLE LAND

Sprays and Fertilisers

A further variation of rear-mounted equipment is the sprayer which comprises a tank that is connected to a wide boom. It is used mainly to dress a growing crop with an appropriate chemical treatment, either against fungal or insect damage, or with a selective weedkiller. As the crop develops, the tractor will pass through the field using prepared tramlines. In order to reduce any physical damage to the crop during this process, a tractor may be fitted with special narrow wheels that spread less across the tramlines but can only be used for light work of this nature under dry conditions. An alternative to this is to have a specialised sprayer with its own built-in power unit running on narrow wheels and constructed so as to give it a greater height clearance over the crop. Such spraying can also be done by air, from a light aircraft or helicopter, thereby avoiding any risk of physical damage to the crop. It is, however, a more expensive option, especially when using a helicopter, and tends not to be as accurate and is therefore likely to be used only on large-scale operations or when ground conditions have prevented any wheeled access.

At an earlier stage in the crop development, a top dressing of fertiliser or of chemicals may be applied by purpose-built tractors running on huge flotation tyres which cause negligible damage to the crop and can furthermore operate at fast speeds. Such equipment is both specialised and expensive and tends to indicate that it belongs to a contractor rather than to the farm itself.

Another such operation that can sometimes be seen taking place on bare land before the new crop has been sown is the injection of fertilising material into the ground. Working in some ways on the same principles as a seed drill, this process is used for the application of sewage sludge, which now also goes under the more modern and euphemistic name of 'biosolids'. This provides considerable manurial benefits for the crop, but, as it could be potentially offensive if spread across the surface of the land, it is often applied directly into the ground. The most basic, or primary, sludge may be

2 ARABLE LAND

applied only to land used for non-food crops such as those grown for conversion into industrial oil, whereas for most ordinary cultivations it will be in a treated (and generally less smelly) form.

The conventional manure spreader is, however, less discreet, although it can still sometimes be recognised as much by its smell as by its appearance! This comprises a tractor-drawn trailer which is fitted with a mounted auger or cannon that can disperse farmyard manure or slurry onto the land. Whilst used equally on arable or grassland, it is seen mostly on dairy and beef farms and is mentioned therefore in a little more detail in Chapter 3.

Subsoiling

Another operation that may be seen on bare land, particularly in areas of heavy soils such as clay, is subsoiling. This involves a rear-mounted series of tines that are worked just below the surface of the ground with the purpose of breaking up the hard pan that can develop either naturally or as a result of the repeated pressure of machinery being driven across the land. This applies especially to the headland which gets extra usage as a turning circle or connecting route to adjacent fields. Whilst the topsoil or surface of the field is worked regularly with the various cultivations mentioned above, the subsoil, which lies generally a few inches below, is also important to the growth of the plants growing above and needs to be kept sufficiently friable to allow for drainage and for root development.

This function may also be carried out with a single tine at the base of which is a bullet-shaped device known appropriately as a mole plough. This is worked at a lower depth than the subsoiler and has the effect of creating a series of narrow tunnels beneath the surface which aid drainage, particularly in clay soils.

As may be imagined, these operations that draw equipment well below the surface of the ground require more mechanical power than other cultivations and therefore use larger tractors and even crawlers.

Heavier soils tend to incorporate an underdrainage system constructed of series of pipes and gravel and assisted sometimes by mole ploughing. The drains themselves remain in working order for many years, depending on the type of land, and their construction is not therefore part of any regular soil maintenance or cultivation work.

Roads and Gateways

Many of the implements described in the preceding sections are designed to work over a wide span so as to give the most efficient coverage of big arable fields. Often these will be too large to either pass through gateways or be transported safely along a road. The necessary manoeuvrability is gained by having a mechanism which enables sections of the implements to be folded up rather like the wings of aeroplanes on an aircraft carrier. They can therefore appear rather differently when being taken along the road than when working out on the field, where the span of a sprayer or roller can extend to between 3 and 6 metres or even 12 metres for the largest models.

Harvesting

Combineable Crops

A whole category of crops has already been referred to as 'combineable' and these are essentially all gathered in by the same process.

Combine Harvesters

The combine harvester will be a familiar sight to all who visit arable parts of the country in the late summer and early autumn. It is a remarkable and complex machine that has done much to transform traditional farming both in Britain and, more significantly, in other parts of the world such as North America. As this book does not aspire to be an agricultural engineering manual, it seems appropriate to focus on what the 'combine' is actually doing when seen out in the fields and also what the reasons might be for the occasions when it is not working even though the harvest appears to be under way. The answer to the last point is, as so often in farming, the weather. Combineable crops such as cereals and oilseeds can generally only be sold or stored successfully if they are sufficiently dry. A wet or damp sample will deteriorate and even heat up unless it is dried or turned. Newly harvested crops are often passed through a drying plant before further handling or storage, but this process has its limitations and adds crucially to the cost of harvesting. There is a limitation also to the condition of crops that can be cut by the combine and it is rare therefore to see a combine working when it is wet, either after it has rained or even in the early mornings before a heavy dew has cleared. Conversely, combines may be out working at night, using headlamps, and this could well signify that a spell of rain has been forecast and that there is only a light evening dew so that

there is every incentive to continue working until the weather breaks. Timing is also crucial to the condition of the crop regardless of its moisture content. It is important, therefore, to gather in a harvest whilst it is properly ripe, rather than risk a deterioration due to a delay during a spell of bad weather. Another problem is that of lodging, which could well happen when a rain storm hits a mature crop, and although modern combine harvesters are remarkably adept at collecting up such flattened ears, there will inevitably be some loss in both yield and quality.

2 ARABLE LAND

Straw Handling

Where the straw has been left behind the combine harvester, it will either be chopped as mentioned above or baled. Straw bales are a familiar sight, not only when they are being made but also because they are often left in the field for some days where they create an almost sculptured effect. The baler is drawn behind a tractor and gathers up each row of straw, compresses it into either a rounded or rectangular bulk, binds it together with twine or a plastic sheet and then drops it either onto the ground or onto a sledge to which it is coupled. Previously, such bales were neat parcels that could still each be lifted by one man. These are still occasionally made, especially where there is demand for them from, for example, horse owners. Improved mechanisation has, however, meant that most bales are now of a much larger size, being about 1.25 metres in diameter and weighing up to as much as 1 tonne depending on the density and crop type, and can only be gathered in by a forklift attachment. Straw bales can be stacked together in the open, either on a field headland or in a yard, and then stored by this means for the winter, although there will be less deterioration and wastage if they can be put in covered accommodation such as in a Dutch barn.

Loaders

Big bales, as they are still known, are moved either by a specialised telescopic handler or by a hydraulic attachment fitted to the front or rear of a tractor. In both cases this will use either a grapple arrangement or simply a single prong that can be speared into the bale sufficiently securely to allow it to be lifted and transported over short distances.

Root Crops

Potatoes, sugar beet and carrots are all harvested by specialist equipment that lifts the crops from beneath the surface and transfers them by a conveyor or elevator to a trailer that is attached to its rear. During this process any extraneous matter, such as earth and stones or pieces of haulm (which are the unwanted tops of the plants), is allowed to fall between the web of the conveyor back onto the ground so that the gathered crop is as

44

2 ARABLE LAND

*Sugar beet being unloaded
from a clamp*

clean as possible. For potatoes and carrots this may involve additionally some manual work, either on the harvester itself or in the yard before the crop is packed or stored. The handling of these two crops throughout is done with care so as not to cause damage to the tubers which would reduce their marketability and storage life. Sugar beet can be more robustly handled, being for processing rather than direct consumption, although it still needs to be cleaned of excess soil. Sugar beet harvesting includes cutting the green tops, which are then either left on the ground and ploughed back in later or collected for livestock feed. Before potatoes are lifted, the haulm is either left to wither or is desiccated with an application of a dilute chemical mix. Carrot tops remain on the crop during harvesting and are even in some methods used in the lifting process. Whilst potatoes and carrots are stored mostly in specialist buildings or packed for sale, sugar beet is stacked temporarily on concrete pads on the roadside prior to being carted to the factory once the processing or 'campaign' gets under way. A traditional method of storing potatoes under an earth mound or clamp can still sometimes be seen, although this is now rare, as it cannot provide the same quality control or frost protection as a modern building.

The Cost of Ownership

The scale and sophistication of many agricultural machines suggests that they are extremely costly and makes one wonder how farmers can afford to own them, especially when some are used only for a few weeks or even days in the year. The answer is that they need not necessarily be owned outright. They may instead be leased or hired or operated by a contractor who, by working for several farmers at a time, is able to make more efficient use of his machinery. Latterly, in the face of declining profits, more farmers have joined together to form co-operatives or machinery 'rings' whereby items of equipment are bought jointly and then used separately by the individual members. Many farms have workshops and are able to carry out repairs and maintenance on their equipment, so that it becomes feasible to retain it for several years or to buy in used machines rather than new ones. Incidentally, when buying a used car, the critical factors are its age

45

and mileage; in the case of self-propelled farm machinery, however, it is the hours that the tractor or combine, for example, has worked that will have been recorded and that are then assessed rather than the mileage.

Prices vary enormously, not only according to the size and type of machine, but with discounts and other incentives. When agricultural incomes decline, farmers feel unable to buy new replacements and tend to make do with their ageing equipment. To the farmer this may save a capital outlay, whilst incurring higher maintenance costs and a greater risk of breakdown. To the machinery dealers, however, it means a downturn in business which may well have to be countered by offering discounts and special deals. Breakdowns can create a hidden cost beyond that of carrying out the repair; if a combine stops in the middle of harvest several hours and even days may be lost before a replacement part can be delivered and installed, during which time the weather may have changed and the crop will then have deteriorated before the harvest can be restarted.

However, whenever one sees a piece of farm equipment at work or on the road, it is intriguing to know what it may have cost. As an indication, one may expect a medium-sized four-wheel drive tractor to be about £30,000. A middle-range combine harvester with a 4-metre cutter bar would be three times that much, at around £90,000. A six-furrow reversible plough could be about £15,000 and a big baler would be about the same price. A small mounted sprayer seems more reasonable at under £2000, but at the other end of the scale a big self-propelled one would cost over £40,000! It is clear that there is a lot of capital committed even to just getting out onto the land.

Work Rates

The sight of a single tractor working meticulously up and down a large open field can make one wonder how long it might take to complete the various cultivations and other tasks. The traditional measure of an acre was originally supposed to represent the amount of land that could be ploughed by a team of oxen in one day. Nowadays, a modern tractor can cover between 8 and 20 acres (or 3 to 8 hectares) in an 8-hour day, depending on the type of land and tractor. Drilling might be done at up to about 1 hectare per hour, whilst spraying rates average at around 4 hectares per hour. Combining depends greatly upon conditions but tends to run at about 1 hectare per hour.

Although farms and estates are still often advertised in terms of acres, most agricultural operations are now measured in metric units, whether as kilograms of seed or tonnes of grain harvest or indeed hectares of land. It is difficult to envisage what a hectare would comprise in the open countryside, especially as field boundaries can be quite irregular, but one convenient comparison is that it is roughly the same as a football pitch. A hectare is almost 2 ½ times an acre which can be envisaged either as a square of 70 by 70 yards or as being equivalent very approximately to six tennis courts.

Implement Sheds

Notwithstanding the considerable cost of machinery, it is a surprising feature of many farms that some implements are not kept under protective cover but are left standing out in the open, either in the yard or even in a corner of a field. This is explained perhaps in part by the cost of providing buildings within which to garage them. As machines have become bigger, they no longer fit into the sheds in which such items would have been stored in the past. There is now probably more equipment on a farm, as agriculture has become increasingly mechanised and less labour intensive. Higher and wider buildings are needed and have often been constructed, either in place of or alongside older barns, but sometimes it has been financially more expedient to resort to a compromise position in which some equipment is left uncovered. There is a growing tendency nonetheless for farmyards now to be kept clear and uncluttered, if only because of the increasing risk that anything left out might easily be stolen. This conflicts perhaps with the traditional image of farms where old bits and pieces seem to be lying around, getting smothered in weeds. This may be a reflection of the lack of storage space, but it is also an indication of differing standards and perceptions. Those who work on the land have to prioritise the essential daily tasks and they may not always have the time or energy to carry out all those other jobs that still remain around the farm at the end of each day, such as doing repairs to buildings or tidying up the yard. Farming can still be a physically demanding business, beset by the unpredictable vagaries of animals and climate and relying on only limited individual resources, so that it faces a different degree of pressure to that experienced by most other forms of work or enterprise.

Sometimes a large roller or harrow is left in a field entrance, away from the farmyard. This is likely to be for the purpose of preventing travellers driving onto farmland and setting up camp there.

Crop Storage

Arable crops are harvested just once a year and there is therefore an intrinsic need to be able to store them and to make them available for gradual use throughout the ensuing 12 months. This can be done in a centralised system of silos, run either by a co-operative or by grain merchants or even, in the case of intervention, by the government. There is, however, a tradition of storing crops on individual farms, in large steel buildings that often form the most noticeable feature of the farmstead. Such on-farm storage has the advantage of reducing transport time at harvest, which can be critical if the crop is not to be spoiled, and also of enabling farmers to retain their produce until they can gain the best price. It is a simple matter of economics to realise that at the actual moment of harvest, prices will be at their lowest and that they should then rise during the ensuing months.

Grain stores tend now to be portal-framed buildings, enclosed in steel or sometimes still asbestos cladding, with load-resistant steel walls to a height of about 2.5 metres. The grain will be stored on a concrete floor or in separate silos; in either case there is likely to be a system of ventilation ducts to allow the crop to be dried and, if necessary, cooled. Handling may be by means of a series of augers or by use of a tractor-mounted bucket. The drier mechanism may sometimes be seen housed against the outside walls of the store in a sort of lean-to construction. There may also be a simple canopy construction with a pit underneath, from which the corn is augered into the store. The purpose of this pit is essentially to facilitate the process of receiving grain into storage from the field. Free-standing circular steel silos are now rare, although a few old ones can still be seen as a reminder of an era when that design provided a practical and economical answer. Over the years, crops yields have increased and harvesting has become speedier, and latterly hygiene standards have become more stringent too, so that storage buildings have had to become more sophisticated. One factor in designing and maintaining such buildings is being able to comply with Crop Assurance Schemes which impose stringent conditions regarding pests such as birds and mice and also contamination.

Grain being stored over ventilation ducts

2 ARABLE LAND

Grain stores, although by their name seemingly suited only for corn, can also be used for other combineable crops such as oilseed and beans. Potatoes, however, are stored separately in buildings that are similar in external appearance to those for grain, although many of them will include internal insulation or a facility for climate control. Potatoes are vulnerable to frost damage and, being destined entirely for the human food markets, there is a need to maintain them in good condition until the point of sale.

Straw bales are best stored in an open-sided portal-framed building, or Dutch barn, as mentioned earlier. These barns were, however, largely erected before the advent of big bales and their design, although clear spanned and high, is not so well suited to the scale of bulk handling that is now involved. Some of the older buildings, such as those with curved corrugated iron roofs, may date from the time when more arable farms also carried livestock. The straw would then be stored close to where the cattle were being housed during the winter, probably near to the centre of the yard, and Dutch barns can still be seen overlooking the heart of a farmstead.

Other Buildings
An arable farm may have a workshop that is likely to be a fully enclosed barn. It may also have a chemical store which has to be totally secure, but is a smaller shed and less noticeable other than by the bright hazard sign posted on the door.

Glasshouses have already been mentioned in connection with horticulture. In the localities where such crops are grown, these buildings can be seen covering quite extensive areas, following a trend towards larger units and higher buildings that let in a greater amount of light. In those districts where potatoes are grown, smaller glasshouses may be seen on the edge of an ordinary farmyard. These are not in fact used for growing crops but are 'chitting houses' in which seed potatoes are stored prior to planting, with the purpose that the light will encourage the early development of new shoots.

2 ARABLE LAND

Most buildings represent a substantial investment on a farm. Many of them will have been constructed some years ago, at a time when such work was even being grant aided, and may have been improved and upgraded in the meantime. Under present circumstances, it would be difficult for an individual farming business to finance such a project and it is rare therefore to see new buildings. Greater use will be made instead of co-operatives and other central arrangements, as is already the case for many of the more specialised crops such as carrots or onions.

Some modern buildings seem to have outgrown the proportions of the traditional farmyard and one wonders how permission was ever given for them to be constructed in such a seemingly insensitive manner. The answer is that until relatively recently, most agricultural buildings did not require planning consent. This was mainly due to the fact that farming was still considered to be a high priority industry and because previously such buildings had rarely been of a noticeable size. They were designed for what would normally have been a family unit, but as farms became bigger, so too did the buildings and the impact that they have on the landscape. Planning regulations do now cover agricultural buildings and often require the use of more sensitive siting and finishing than had been the case, especially for the larger buildings. Also, as it happens, there have been far fewer new farm buildings erected in the recent times of falling incomes.

Irrigation

It has already been mentioned that many root and vegetable crops need to be grown in light land so that they can be harvested more easily and more reliably. This is often in the eastern side of the country where the rainfall is less, but even in, say, the Vale of Evesham in Worcestershire the ground will still tend to dry out in a warm summer due to its particular qualities. The crops are then sustained by irrigation which is often quite eye-catching in the flat open countryside where such crops are grown. This is either by

means of a water canon swivelling automatically in arcs across the land or
from a gantry that is wheeled along the fields, again under its own water
power. At a time of increasing domestic and industrial demand for water,
agricultural irrigation is carefully controlled by licences that determine not
only the quantity but also the timing of what may be applied. The water is
extracted from bore holes or open ditches on the farm, although large
lagoons looking almost like ornamental lakes can now often be seen within
these arable areas. These will have been constructed for the purpose of
retaining water in the winter and using it for irrigation in the summer when
it would otherwise be restricted.

Irrigation can only be warranted on crops and soil types that really require
it and where premium prices can be obtained for the produce. Cereals can
come under 'stress' during dry periods and then become stunted or ripen
prematurely, whether on light or heavy land. However, the response to
irrigation would be limited and the ordinary market prices obtained from
these crops would not justify the added cost of irrigation.

It is possible to see what looks like irrigation equipment at work over
grassland and this will in fact be spreading slurry rather than water, as
explained in Chapter 3.

3 GRASSLAND

This chapter deals with fields and meadows that are under grass but which lie within cultivated areas of the country as opposed to hill land which is described in the next section.

The Seasons

The different seasons are less evident in grassland than in the arable areas where the landscape changes from bare soil to young plants to ripening crops and then to harvested stubbles, although there are certainly variations to be noted.

In winter the fields are largely empty of livestock, especially on dairy farms where all the cows and most of the other cattle will be kept under cover. This is mainly because the grass is not growing and because the land would be liable to become damaged or 'poached' if the cattle were to be left in the fields during wet wintry weather when it rarely gets the chance to dry out. The animals themselves would be able to withstand being out during such weather, but they would lose condition and require more feed in order not only to maintain their body weight but also to continue to produce milk. One of the welcome signs of spring is therefore not just the greening of the hedges or the emergence of the daffodils, but the fact that the landscape is dotted again with grazing cows!

Sheep on the other hand are frequently left out to graze throughout the winter, as they do less damage to the land and, with the provision of extra feed, can sustain themselves sufficiently well. Pregnant ewes will now often be brought under cover for lambing and then be let out into the fields again once their offspring are strong enough and when conditions allow. Traditionally, this would have been a sign of spring, although in lowland areas they may be seen already in the late winter, as any opportunity to rear lambs early will gain a premium price in the markets.

3 GRASSLAND

Grazing continues for all livestock until the end of autumn, although during the early summer the animals will be excluded from certain fields which are then left to grow more thickly until they are cut for hay or silage. Hay tends to be harvested just once a year in the early summer when the grass has reached its best condition for this purpose. Silage, on the other hand, may be cut two or even three times in the season. Once these forage harvests are completed, the land can be opened up again for grazing until the shorter days and wetter weather mean that the stock must return to their yards.

Grass is no longer the only crop that is conserved for winter fodder and there are some others that are grown as arable crops, notably forage maize for silage or turnips for winter grazing. This then brings another seasonal aspect to grassland farms, with land being ploughed, cultivated and harvested.

Permanent Pasture and Leys

Much of the grass seen in the lowland landscape will in fact have been grown as a crop, rather than just maintained continually as a meadow from year to year. For this, the land will have been ploughed and cultivated and sown with grass seed. This produces a temporary grass or 'ley' that will be retained either as a short ley for perhaps two or three years or as a long ley, which may be between five or ten years, according to circumstances. The main rationale for doing this is twofold: firstly, to rejuvenate a pasture in which unproductive grasses and weeds are beginning to predominate; and secondly, to be able to exploit for an arable crop the fertility that has built up from the land having previously been grazed. This fertility arises largely from the dung and urine of the grazing animals and from the spreading of farmyard manure or slurry and partly from the nitrogen held in the soil, especially where the pasture included clover, as mentioned below. Growing grass intermittently within an otherwise arable system allows also for the

3 GRASSLAND

land to be cleared of those weeds and diseases that affect arable crops and are more difficult to eradicate when under more continuous cropping.

Old undisturbed grassland, or 'permanent pasture', can be identified by the fact that there is likely to be a greater mix of grass varieties and probably also of traditional weeds such as buttercup. The ley is of a more

consistent appearance and most weeds will have been controlled or eradicated as part of the establishment process. Permanent pastures will have been left undisturbed where the ground may be too wet to plough or reseed successfully, as in the case of river meadows, or where there is a policy of conservation or simply for reasons of tradition.

On occasions, signs of the old ridge and furrow dating from the Middle Ages can still be seen. Now looking rather like waves in the grassland, these parallel mounds were formed by the regular ploughing under the medieval strip system whereby the soil was raised into a broad central ridge. This not only allowed the different strips to be delineated but also meant that, in an era before tile drains were invented, water could run off the land more readily down the intervening furrows. These patterns were therefore preserved in later years, particularly on heavier land where such drainage would have been crucial. Thereafter this heavy land might have been given over to grass as other lighter soils were used for arable cultivation instead, and the old ridge and furrow has remained virtually undisturbed ever since. Elsewhere, as the land remained in arable use and was then able to benefit from improved drainage, the ridges would have been ploughed out and been lost from view.

Some of the more modern and productive grasses do have a distinctive appearance, not just in close detail but in overall colour, so that the presence of leys in the landscape can sometimes be identified by the stronger shade of green.

Grass Types

Grasses are in the main much more difficult to identify than arable crops, not least because they have fewer discernible features. The most predominant types are the ryegrasses, which are partly indigenous, like perennial ryegrass, and partly introduced, such as Italian ryegrass, and which may be sown as a mixture with modern strains of other old varieties, notably timothy and cocksfoot. Clover, with its distinctive red or white flowers and three-sided leaves, is also included in some seed mixes both for its nutritional value to livestock and for its ability to fix atmospheric nitrogen into the soil.

Grass Seed

With such a widespread requirement for seed for leys, some farmers grow grass as a crop to be harvested for seed. This may be evident when a grass field is left standing rather than cut for hay or silage and is then gathered in through a version of a combine harvester rather than a mower or forage harvester. The production of grass seed is very exacting as it needs to be kept free of weeds and common grasses and so the crop may well be noticeable by its pristine appearance!

Forage Cropping

Hay

Traditionally, grass will have been not only grazed throughout the growing season but also conserved for the winter in the form of hay. When cut under the right conditions and then dried before storage, hay can provide a nutritional feed for most forms of livestock, particularly still for horses and sheep. The drying occurs generally in the field; the grass that has been cut by a mower can be seen lying in rows and changing colour to a lighter green or yellow. To aid the drying process these rows or 'swaths' may need to be turned by a tedder to allow better circulation of air. Once the moisture content has been reduced sufficiently, these swaths are then gathered up in a baler and carted into a barn or covered area. For hay to be

Hay being turned and baled

3 GRASSLAND

stored successfully throughout the winter, it is crucial that it is allowed to dry sufficiently before baling as it will otherwise become mouldy or even combust. Even if, after a period of wet weather, the hay has finally been worked down to a low enough degree of moisture to be stored safely, the quality and nutritional value will have deteriorated significantly, due to the time delay and the additional handling. In the grass-growing areas of western Britain that are prone to rain at the best of times, even in June, one can see that hay making can be hard work and even heartbreaking!

Hay can also be dried in a barn, in a similar way to the combineable crops, but in most cases the costs of doing so make it uneconomical for ordinary livestock production. Unlike grain drying which is installed on most cereal farms, barn driers for hay are rather specialised and unlikely therefore to be available as a resource that farmers could turn to in times of bad weather. Another forage crop that benefits from barn drying to produce a nutritious feed is lucerne, or alfalfa, although this is grown relatively rarely in this country compared to other parts of the world where grass is less abundant. Lucerne is a legume and not a grass and has a light leafy plant with a small pale flower not unlike a pea. It is more likely to be seen in areas of lighter land, being deep rooted and therefore able to withstand drought.

Hay and straw may look alike especially when baled up, but there are some easy clues for telling the two apart. In the field, it is firstly a matter of season; hay is best made in the early summer whereas straw follows the cereal harvest in the autumn. Also, hay bales are less likely to be seen left out on the land as the potential loss in condition from rain is greater than with straw, which is sometimes only gathered in once other priorities have been fulfilled. Hay bales will be on ground that is green with the new growth of grass whereas straw will be among stubbles through which the bare earth would be showing, amongst of course a certain amount of weed and regenerated grain. There is, however, one situation where one might be confused by seeing straw bales standing on grass and that is when the

3 GRASSLAND

arable crop is being followed by a ley and the grass has been 'undersown'. As the name implies, this involves sowing the grass seed into the cereal crop in the spring and allowing it to develop beneath the canopy of that crop so that it is fully established once the harvest has been taken in the autumn. Close to, hay has a much softer texture than straw which has a thicker and more prickly stalk, often not unlike a drinking straw. Both may be baled in a large round or rectangular bale, held together with a light plastic netting or twine. Smaller rectangular bales are also still seen, especially for hay, as these are easier to handle without heavy machinery by smallholders or horse owners.

Although one of the clues mentioned above is that hay tends to be made in the early summer, it can still be seen later in the season too, if it has been left to grow again for a second cut. On occasions hay might be seen being made even later in the year, at around the time of the cereal harvest. This will be according to circumstance, such as on smaller fields and at times when the price of hay is low. However, when hay is left like that it loses some of its feed value and for that reason it is usually cut and baled at an earlier stage, before the seed heads have formed on the grass. Even when grass is being grazed late in the year and may still look lush and green, it will have less nutritional value and cows will then begin to be given an additional feed such as cereal to supplement their diet.

Silage

An alternative form of grass conservation has been developed in more recent times which overcomes many of the uncertainties of hay making and produces a palatable feed for dairy cows and also beef cattle and sheep. It has now become a familiar sight in the summer countryside as it is made within those large rolls of black or pale green or white plastic that are lined up across the fields. Silage is a process where the grass is cut and then stored under airtight conditions which allow it to ferment to a controlled degree and then remain in a stable and palatable state throughout the winter. The original method for doing this, which is still widely used,

involves collecting the grass as it is cut into a high-sided trailer, rather like an oversize lawn mower, and then carting it to a large open bunker or 'clamp' in the farmyard. Here it is unloaded and compacted down and then covered with a seal of black plastic sheeting, which is then held in place generally with a collection of old tyres. Again, this is a rather familiar if unattractive rural sight! Old tyres are, however, readily available – being difficult to dispose of by other means – and they provide an efficient method of securing the black plastic and are easy to move as the clamp begins to be used.

As winter arrives and the cows have had to come off the grassland, the silage clamp is opened at the front and then either cut and carted to feeding troughs in the yard or offered for grazing in situ. The silage has by then a light brown colour or, if of poorer quality, it may be rather darker and have a slightly slimy appearance. It has an almost sweet smell and the cows take to it readily. When silage is made in a clamp, the fermentation process produces a rather acrid black liquid or effluent that can be damaging to organisms in water courses and therefore has to be drained off and disposed of safely. The presence of such effluent, which is harmless to the livestock, can be reduced or even avoided if the silage is wilted, by being allowed to dry in the field before it is stored. This wilting procedure has to be used in any event when the grass is baled up in plastic and is the reason that lines of cut grass can be seen on the ground.

Cut silage being wilted

The process of wilting can, however, have the effect of reducing the bulk and quality of the silage and needs to be done as quickly as possible if losses are to be avoided. Nevertheless it usually takes a day or two. It involves therefore, as so often in farming, a risk of a delay due to bad weather, faulty machinery or overworked contractors that will result in a poorer crop. It is possible to compensate for some of these losses and to improve the overall condition of the silage by putting additives such as molasses, bacteria or a dilute acid into the finished silage.

3 GRASSLAND

Forage maize

Silage is most commonly made from grass, especially when being done in the summer or when it is being baled. There are, however, occasions when forage harvesters may be seen in the late autumn working through a tall and rather dry-looking crop which will be maize. Known to us in other forms as sweet corn and as the ingredient for cornflakes or popcorn, most of the maize grown in this country is for cattle feed in the form of silage, since it is only in the southernmost areas that varieties for human consumption can be expected to ripen. Unlike the grain maize for human foodstuffs, where only the ear is harvested, when making silage the complete plant is used and chopped leaving a field of cut stalks. These stubbles are sometimes left to be grazed by sheep or as cover for game birds.

Just occasionally, too, the forage harvesters will be at work in the early summer in a crop that although green seems too tall and bulky for grass. This is for 'whole crop' silage that is made from a specially sown mix of cereals which is then cut and ensiled just like grass but which then

3 GRASSLAND

produces the advantage of a higher nutritional content. Lucerne, or alfalfa, which was mentioned in the preceding section on hay, can also be cut for silage but is only rarely used in this country.

The plastic-covered bales of grass silage are very noticeable, and rather unattractive, when left in the field, even those using the newer and lighter coloured material. Ultimately they are likely to be moved to a standing near to where the cows are being kept and then stacked together, so as to make them most easily available for feeding. However, since the plastic gives such complete protection to the crop within it, there is not the same need to get the bales under cover as with, for example, conventional hay bales and the task of moving them is often postponed until other more pressing jobs have been attended to. Nonetheless, if they are left in the open, there is a risk of the plastic being pecked by crows which then allows air to get in and spoil the silage.

Zero Grazing

The name of this system seems to suggest that the cattle get nothing to eat, but in fact it involves the grass being cut and brought to them in a yard or open enclosure! It is not commonly used in Britain, as it is better suited to countries with larger farms and landscapes, notably the USA. However, as herds increase in size in the UK it is possible that one will see grass and other forage crops being cut and carted to the cows throughout the growing season and not just at hay or silage-making times.

Turf

There is one type of grassland where instead of the crop being grazed or cut it may be dug up and carted away! It will in fact be a non-agricultural variety that has been grown for turf and which can be lifted by a purpose-built cutting machine and rolled into short bundles. This was previously a very specialised process, but it is now becoming more

3 GRASSLAND

widespread. The increase in new housing developments and the growing fashion for gardening has created a significant demand for making instant lawns. The technique for cutting, or stripping, turf has been refined to such an extent that only a very thin layer of soil is lifted with the grass. This reduces the potential damage to the land itself and makes the product less heavy to handle whilst still, apparently, allowing the grass to survive the transportation and to take root in its new location. The land from which it has been cut will then probably be reseeded and cultivated for a further crop. A field being grown for turf can be noticeable not only because of the cutting and previously sometimes the mowing too, but also because it is about the only occasion when grassland may be seen being irrigated.

In Ireland, turf would refer to cutting peat, traditionally for fuel and now for garden compost. There are areas in Britain where peat has been harvested for compost but this is now strictly limited for ecological reasons.

Grassland Management

As grass is not grown afresh each year like an arable crop, it does not involve the same annual process of cultivation, although there are still a number of regular tasks that need to be done throughout the season.

To begin with, after winter, some pastures may look rather like a large well-mown lawn as a pattern of wide stripes appears across the fields. The pattern is the result of rolling, which compacts the earth that may have been lifted by the frost. This prevents the roots from being loosened and also avoids soil being gathered up with the silage.

Perversely, one may also see what appears to be just the opposite process being carried out over grassland at this same time of year. A chain harrow drawn systematically across the field like a giant mat of spikes helps to break up tangled clumps of grass, especially in older pastures, and to aerate the soil and roots. Whether the land is rolled or harrowed will depend on the type of land, the severity of the winter and the condition of the pasture. Harrowing can also be used to help spread molehills and farmyard manure, as mentioned below.

As temperatures begin to rise in the spring and as the grass starts to grow again, it may be dressed with a granular fertiliser. This would be applied from a hopper mounted on the back of a tractor and fitted with a mechanised dispenser that broadcasts the fertiliser out across a swathe of the field. Farmyard manure will also occasionally have been applied earlier on, before the livestock are turned out to graze, as a means both of adding fertility to the land and of disposing of the inevitable by-product of keeping a herd of animals under cover all winter! Muck spreading is usually done out of a tractor-drawn trailer that has an auger fitted horizontally at the rear, from which the manure is then shovelled out onto the land. There are also larger, purpose-built, self-powered machines which are rather specialised and likely therefore to be operated by contractors. Such equipment is able to work more rapidly than conventional trailers which are limited in size and tend to use up time in having to travel to and from the farmyard in order to be refilled. The bigger machines will often be fitted with extra large tyres to enable them to carry these heavier loads without creating wheel ruts and thereby damaging the pasture. Another way of limiting such damage is to do the work during a frost, creating the rather incongruous sight of dark manure being spread onto a sparkling white surface!

There are cattle systems, as described in Chapter 4, which do not use straw bedding and where the manure is in the form of a liquid slurry that is again carted onto the fields in special tanker trailers and spread onto the land. Slurry can also be pumped on to the land through an arrangement of pipes leading to a water cannon which may be seen (and smelt!) shooting out the contents in a circling arc over the fields.

3 GRASSLAND

On grassland these operations will always be using exclusively farmyard slurry; the sewage sludge or biosolids referred to in Chapter 2 cannot be applied on forage that is going to be fed directly to animals, as it can contain elements that would be unsuitable for ingestion but which are effectively neutralised in the arable process.

By the time the summer comes, livestock farmers are involved in hay and silage making, as already mentioned, but can also be seen carrying out regular management tasks on the pasture such as topping and fencing.

Topping is the cutting of those larger weeds that the stock do not eat, notably thistles, docks and nettles, generally by a tractor-mounted rotary mower. Once cut and left on the ground, these weeds become more palatable and may yet be eaten by sheep or cattle, but the main purpose of topping is to prevent them from spreading, especially through seeding.

Cows strip grazing kale

Fencing work can be either repairing or renewing permanent post and wire fences or moving temporary electric ones. The former may involve a tractor-mounted post hole borer, looking like a giant corkscrew, and also a hand-operated ratchet for straining the wire while it is stapled to the posts. Electric fencing is used mostly for boundaries that are moved on a daily or possibly seasonal basis. For cows, this will be just a single strand of wire held in place by slender metal or plastic posts at a height that coincides approximately with the nose of a grazing cow. At one end is a small battery or mains transformer producing a 12-volt current that is just sufficient to give a slight warning shock to any animal (or roaming human!) that brushes against it. Such fences are used mostly for strip grazing, whereby the cows are restricted to one section of fresh pasture at any one time and are prevented from going over the entire field, since that could result in less efficient usage with some areas being trampled down or spoiled with dung. They may not be very visible from a distance, other than that there is likely to be a clear distinction within the field between lush dark green grazing on one side and more yellowed and muddied ground on the other!

3 GRASSLAND

Sheep are also enclosed by such temporary fencing when it is necessary to conserve part of their pasture or when they are brought onto arable stubbles or winter forage crops, such as turnips. There may be occasions too when they are brought into paddocks that have been used by horses or cattle who do not graze so closely as sheep and therefore leave some useful foraging. Sheep have a great ability to push through hedges and fences that were designed to restrain larger animals and which therefore have to be supplemented by a run of wire netting or electric fencing. In this case, the fence is again held in place by insulated stakes but takes the form of an electrified netting or a double strand of wire, since a single strand could be easily passed over by sheep.

The same can apply to pigs when they are brought either out onto land where an arable crop has been grown, for which no fencing was needed, or onto a grass field.

Grassland is still frequently bounded or enclosed by hedges and these need trimming every year or so, partly to prevent them becoming too large and partly to ensure that they remain compact and thick enough not to be breached by livestock. This is generally done in the late summer or autumn when there is more time available and when the hedgerow trees and plants will have stopped growing for the year. As so many of our hedges run along road verges, the process may be quite a familiar sight with a tractor and side-mounted flail slashing away their tops and sides. The immediate result may not look very picturesque, but it is effective and economical, and luckily by the following spring the worst of the scars will have grown over. The more traditional method of laying a hedge by hand is still to be seen in certain areas and is again being encouraged and revived. There is further mention of hedges and fences in Chapter 7.

All livestock when grazing will require water, especially the cattle, and the simplest means of providing this is where there happens to be a river or stream running along the pasture. In such situations the animals will

3 GRASSLAND

normally have free access to the water's edge, although that might have to be controlled or restricted were it to cause undue erosion of the river banks. Occasionally, old dew ponds can be seen which would have been dug out in an otherwise dry area with the purpose of catching dew and rain and thereby providing water for the stock. A more modern and usual method is, however, by means of underground pipes laid to each of the grass fields and supplying a galvanised or plastic trough. These are normally to be seen on the edge of fields or even within a boundary hedge from where one trough can be accessed from either of the adjoining pastures. The supply is then controlled by a ballcock valve (such as is used in lavatory cisterns), which allows the water to be replenished automatically whenever the level falls, whether through being consumed or by evaporation. These water supplies may be off the mains and measured by meters or from a private source such as a spring on the farm itself.

Drainage is a regular feature of grassland management, especially in areas of higher rainfall, heavier soils and level or low-lying land. Although grass may look like a natural product, its growth and content will be affected by adverse conditions such as the roots being waterlogged. In some instances this cannot be avoided, as in the case of water meadows that adjoin a stream, or it will even have been encouraged for conservation reasons. One common sign of a wet pasture is the presence of reeds and rushes that are unpalatable to most livestock and will therefore have been left standing as a kind of evidence of the reduced productivity! However, when the grass is being grown for commercial farming, steps will be taken wherever possible to avoid this loss of condition by ensuring that any excess water is allowed to flow off the land. One basic factor in drainage is likely to be the open ditches that run along field boundaries or beside hedges. These will be dug out in winter either by means of a bucket grab, operated hydraulically from the back of a tractor, or with a more specialised digger running on crawler tracks. The spoil from this may then be spread across the headland and probably reseeded with grass in the following spring.

Traditionally, the spoil from a freshly dug ditch would have been used as the base upon which the hedge would then grow. This can often still be seen and is even used as evidence in determining the exact line of a boundary between two properties. The presumption is that farmers would have dug the ditch on the far side of the hedgeline which would then act as a barrier to prevent their own livestock from going into, or across, the ditch.

4 LIVESTOCK

Cattle

Strictly speaking, the term 'cattle' covers all the bovines, including cows, calves, bulls, steers and heifers, but in practice it could be used to refer to the younger stock or the beef herds as distinct from the dairy cows.

Cows

In contrast to the arable world where crop varieties are being constantly developed and diversified, dairying seems to have reverted to one dominant type: the familiar black and white cow or Holstein Friesian. In times gone by, there was a richer variety of different types of cattle, some of which now hardly exist while others are being bred more for special purposes like showing rather than for commercial milk production. Some of these might come under the category of 'rare breeds' and may be seen as attractions on farm visitor enterprises. Previously, however, cows would have been chosen according to their ability to thrive in local conditions, as is still implied in names such as Welsh Black, Galloway, Lincoln Red and Ayrshire. In those days, too, most herds would have been 'dual purpose', with an equal emphasis on the cows producing milk and their male offspring being reared for beef. In recent times, the priority for dairy herds has been more on milk production, with the better quality beef being derived largely from other types of cattle whose characteristics are more suited for that purpose. Meanwhile, grass varieties have been developed so as to produce a better standard of pasture in a wider range of situations, such as on the hills where previously livestock would have had to contend with a poor quality of pasture. Similarly, certain strains of cattle have been improved through breeding to give a higher level of performance under, again, a wider range of conditions. As a result, the black and white cow, or Holstein Friesian is seen not only throughout the British Isles but also in such diverse locations as Africa, the Middle East and its home ground of Canada.

This trend is not, however, universal and happily one does still see a variety of stock around the country. An example of this is found in the lovely

4 LIVESTOCK

dun-coloured Channel Island breeds of Jerseys and Guernseys whose purpose is to produce milk that has more cream, or 'butter fat', than that given by the Friesians and which is still in demand despite modern dietary trends towards less rich foods. Another instance can still be seen, particularly in south west Scotland, in the brown and white markings of the local Ayrshire breed. There may be good grounds, too, for keeping a dual purpose herd and, indeed, there are times when farmers who run specialist dairy breeds find it difficult to sell the male calves as they are unlikely to produce the type and quality of meat required by the market. Another situation when a more colourful diversity of cattle may be seen together is in a beef herd, as referred to later in this chapter.

Dairy cows, as mentioned earlier, are only seen out in the fields between about April and October, depending on which area of the country they are in and on how wet each spring or autumn turns out to be. The size of the herds that are grazing is determined very much according to circumstance, not only as to the available area of pasture land and building accommodation but also as to the labour force committed to it. The minimum number that would be viable as a unit run by one full-time person has increased over the years and is now probably around 100. It is not unusual, however, to have herds of twice this number and even above, as certain dairy farms become increasingly commercial and well equipped. The milk sector enjoyed a period of stability and profitability during much of the twentieth century under the regulation of the Milk Marketing Board (MMB) and especially so after 1983 when a system of quotas was introduced by the European Commission. More recently, however, milk prices in the UK have fallen dramatically following the abolition of the MMB in 1997 and the industry is having to restructure in order to remain viable. This is likely to lead to fewer dairy farms but larger herds. The main limiting factor on herd size is the amount of grassland or other forage area needed to sustain each cow, which tends to be around 1 hectare.

Cows remain in the herd for three or four years or 'lactations', or sometimes

4 LIVESTOCK

longer, before being sold on from the herd, depending on their general condition. These 'cull' cows would previously have been bought by farmers with small herds or otherwise been destined for the food processing industry. However, since the BSE (Bovine Spongiform Encephalopathy) outbreak, regulations have been introduced to reduce the risk of any further contamination so that any beast that is over 30 months old is removed from the food process and has to be incinerated rather than slaughtered for meat production, with the farmer being compensated by the government under a fixed rate according to weight.

Cows are essentially robust creatures but they do need to be able to graze, which requires good feet and teeth! As they grow older, they may lose condition and, being out in all weathers, they are prone also to becoming lame. Being milked each day makes the cows vulnerable to mastitis, which is another common ailment. This can, however, be readily corrected with antibiotics. Bovine tuberculosis is also a serious problem, which has been increasing in incidence in recent years, especially in the south west of England and the West Midlands, and has been publicised from time to time due to the fact that it is linked to badgers. Some conditions are countered with a policy of eradication and are therefore only rarely found, although of these brucellosis does still occur causing abortions among the cows. Foot and mouth disease and anthrax are well-known names, but have both happily not arisen now for many years. BSE, on the other hand, has received much publicity in recent times and caused much concern, not least because of the possibility of it passing to humans. Consequently, it appears now to have been successfully contained and one would certainly not expect to see the symptoms of this 'mad cow disease'. There might be rare instances when cows could sway about and appear decidedly unwell, but these are more likely to be cases of 'staggers' or of 'milk fever' which arise from a temporary deficiency in calcium and minerals and are easily remedied. Indeed, one sign of preventive measures being taken for these is when a slab of a mineral 'lick' is placed in the pastures which the cows and youngstock then taste from time to time.

4 LIVESTOCK

There are countless ways of judging a cow's condition, but a straight back and good proportions and a large udder are some of the essential signs, and seeing one that has become rather boney and seemingly thin is more a measure of age than of lack of fitness. On most farms the cows are milked twice per day, early in the morning and mid- or late afternoon. By and large they become used to the routine and allow themselves to be led quietly into the farmyard. Indeed, at times of good grazing and high production, when the milk builds up and extends their udders, they can become quite keen to get on with it and will bring themselves to the yard without much prompting! With some of the larger and more commercial herds, milking might be done three times daily as a means of spreading the workload, improving performance and reducing the risk of injury or disease. In those cases, one of the milking shifts would be done at night. As a general rule, one cow may produce between about 6000 and 8000 litres of milk and one calf each year, with the occasional twins too.

One thing that may catch the eye when seeing cows around the farm is their means of identification. The stout plastic collars that they wear carry an identification number, and the letters and numbers that may be branded on their backsides are also for identification. It would be difficult otherwise within a commercial herd to tell the cows apart just by sight. It is important to be able to distinguish them for management purposes, particularly regarding medication, calving and feeding. The collars may be fitted with a transponder that can be read electronically as the cows come in for milking so that the rations that they are then fed will be automatically measured out according to the prescribed needs of each individual animal. The branded numbers are, however, read off by the person doing the milking, which is why they are positioned as they are since it is the rear view that is presented to the herdsman when the cows are standing in the parlour! The tags that are clipped into each ear are another means of identification and are in fact now required by regulation, following the BSE crisis. Every cow therefore carries an individual number that can be cross-referenced to its own 'passport' from which its history can be traced as it moves between farms and ultimately to the slaughter house. Gone are the days when cows would be known affectionately by names such as Daisy and Buttercup!

Few dairy cows have horns now and indeed these are superfluous in a domesticated environment such as a lowland farm where there is little need for cows to defend themselves or their calves or to fight for territory and where they would only be likely to cause injury to each other or to the stockmen. In many cases, cattle breeding has evolved a hornless or 'polled' cow, but where this is not the case, the growing point of the horns will be anaesthetically 'debudded' while the calves are still young.

The cash value of a cow varies enormously according to circumstances, but may average out at around £500 to £800, falling to £200 or so at the end of her commercial lactation.

Calves and Followers

There is a further distinction to be noticed between a beef and dairy herd, other than that of variety as mentioned earlier, in that with the latter only the cows will be seen out grazing as the calves are kept separately. They will have been weaned at the earliest reasonable moment; they are separated from the mother at birth or within the first few days and then fed automatically or by bucket on milk or milk substitute until they are able to take cereal concentrates at about five or six weeks. During this time they are housed in individual pens or strawed yards until they are old enough to graze for themselves, which will depend on the time of year at which they were born. Cows calve just once a year and conventionally this takes place in either the spring or autumn, according to circumstance and policy, although many herds do now have an all-year-round calving pattern. One factor in determining this is that cows produce their greatest amount of milk after calving and the price per litre tends to be higher in the autumn and winter than in the early summer. Cows will produce generally one calf but sometimes also twins.

Cows with identification collars feeding on silage

4 LIVESTOCK

As the calves approach maturity, they are known as 'followers' or 'young stock'. These will be the females, or 'heifers', which are destined to join the dairy herd at the age of about two years when they are old enough to have their own calves and to start producing milk. Where these home-bred progeny are kept as replacements for the older cows, it is known as a closed or self-contained herd, although there is also an alternative system where the female calves or heifers are sold and others are then brought in to bring some new blood into the herd. There are two easy ways to determine whether a group of cattle are dairy cows or heifers. Firstly, the heifers are of a slighter build, look younger and do not yet have fully developed udders. Secondly, they may often be seen grazing in fields that are some distance from the homestead rather than in the main pasture areas, as they do not need to be brought into the yard for milking every day.

The male calves may either be sold off soon after birth or otherwise retained and fattened up as 'steers' for beef, even though they may not be of a type best suited for that purpose. For this they will have been castrated when young, partly because by that means they produce a more popular quality of meat and partly also because they can then be retained until they are older. Alternatively, they may be kept as bull beef on a more intensive feeding system and go for slaughter at around 12 or 14 months. As to whether such animals grazing out in the fields might turn out to be bulls rather than steers is discussed in the next section.

Bulls

Confusing as the terminology may be, especially in a book explaining the rudiments of agriculture, on most dairy farms bulls come in the form of straws! This refers to the way in which artificial insemination is applied to the cows. There are two main reasons why this system is now widely used; firstly, it allows farmers to choose exactly what strain they wish to introduce to their herds, as a means of optimising performance; and secondly, it avoids the need to keep a bull on the farm. Bulls are legendary for their ferocity and although in practice they rarely fulfil this reputation, they can

4 LIVESTOCK

Charolais bull

be difficult to manage, especially those from dairy breeds, and have to be kept mostly in specially constructed pens. When a bull is seen out in the fields, it may be for one of three reasons: (1) he is 'running' with the dairy cows or heifers in order to earn his keep; (2) he is part of a suckler herd as described later; or (3) he is not a bull at all! A steer or heifer can appear surprisingly menacing when seen close to, even though its approach is usually only out of curiosity. A bull will still often have a ring in his nose, just as traditionally pictured, since this provides a useful way of handling an animal of that size and temperament which can otherwise be difficult to control. When in the field, he would be expected to look after up to about 40 'wives'.

One is unlikely in fact to encounter a dairy bull in the open, as it is illegal for them to be kept in any field through which there is a footpath. If such a situation does occur, it will be either that the animal is less than 10 months old or that he is of a beef breed (which one must believe to be of a more docile nature!) and is together with the cows and heifers. Strangely, a bull is far less likely to react against a human when he is with the rest of the herd than when he is on his own. A cow with a calf on the other hand can show a more determined spirit if she has reason to feel that her offspring is being threatened, such as by a visiting dog or stranger.

Cattle are normally non-aggressive and not at all dangerous, other than from their sheer weight and momentum if they start to frisk towards someone. When they are grazing close to a footpath, therefore, it is worth keeping an eye on them, staying away from young calves and being ready just to shoo them away if they do get too close for comfort!

Suckler Herds and Beef Cattle
In contrast to the dairy cows, where the stock tends to be so much of the same type and age, there are also herds that are more diverse in age and type. These are suckler herds in which, as the name implies, the cows nurse their calves until they wean themselves onto the grass around them.

4 LIVESTOCK

Under the right conditions, these cows may nurture twins or have an additional calf fostered onto them, under a 'multiple' as opposed to 'single suckler' system. This progeny will be destined for beef or for further breeding, according to their sex, and the cows will be crossed with one of a range of beef bulls, whose colouring varies from, for example, the stone white of Charolais or the chestnut of the Limousin to the brown-red of Hereford or the black Welsh. The herds can therefore show a fine mix of colours as well as of age groups. In the lowlands, they are often kept on land that is unsuited to dairying, such as old or inaccessible meadows and this can also add to the charm. In fact, suckler herds are more commonplace in the hills where conditions no longer favour dairying. Beef produced in this way attracts a premium, due to the quality of the meat and also through special support under the European grant system, that is not generally available for beef reared from dairy calves.

Once weaned, beef cattle are fattened either within yards or on grass, according to the season and the circumstances. The stores, as they are known, are 'finished' at around any age up to 30 months old when they are sold for slaughter. This can be a rather long time to wait for a return, compared to the daily output of milk from a dairy herd which is paid for on a monthly basis. When beef prices are modest, such as after the crisis over BSE, raising cattle in this way is not particularly profitable and is probably done largely in order to make use of some area of old pasture or existing buildings and justified also by the availability of subsidies. If such cattle are housed in buildings during the winter they will be fed predominantly silage supplemented with cereal concentrates.

The most commercial method involves keeping the cattle, especially those originating from a dual purpose dairy herd, in strawed yards for their entire life and feeding them with cereal concentrates or silage throughout the 12 to 14 month period.

4 LIVESTOCK

Beef cattle, like dairy cows, carry two compulsory ear tags with identical numbers, but do not need to be recognised on a daily basis like in a dairy herd and do not therefore usually have any other identification marks. Accurate records do, however, have to be kept of their movements if they are to qualify for grant aid through Beef and Slaughter Premiums.

Cattle Feed

The catastrophic outbreak of BSE in 1998 was traced to an infection in the concentrated feed that was being given to cattle at the time. This caused an understandable sense of outrage about the fact that herbivores such as cows were being fed on rations that contained meat and bone taken from the carcasses of other cattle. The problem, however, lay more in the fact that this meat had not been adequately sterilised rather than that it was wrong or inappropriate to incorporate such ingredients into their feed. Sheep and cattle need to maintain their condition, and output, throughout the winter when there is no fresh grass available and when they are relying otherwise on conserved feed such as silage or hay. Cattle in particular would suffer if they were not provided with some supplements to their diet of silage or treated straw, particularly in the modern context of high performance, relatively high stocking densities and high standards of welfare. Such supplements are provided in a variety of ways, generally in the form of dry pellets, and include cereal grains and grain by-products such as brewers' malt, molassses, oilseeds and legumes, trace minerals and animal products.

4 LIVESTOCK

This last category comprised fish meal and meat and bone meal, each of which provided an efficient source of protein. In some ways, giving fish meal to farm animals could be comparable to humans taking cod liver oil as an effective and natural health supplement. The impression that many people gained of farmers being rather penny pinching and cavalier in feeding their stock with unsuitable material is therefore not quite fair. The principle of feeding meat and bone meal, whilst perhaps rather unattractive, was nonetheless a valid one for providing the required nutrition. The problem lay in the risks now known to be attached to the way in which it was processed and, as a consequence, meat meal and meat and bone meal are now banned throughout Europe as feedstuffs for ruminants.

Sheep

Ewes

Sheep are more of a feature in the hills, as mentioned in Chapter 5, but they are also to be found extensively in lowland districts too where there are distinctive breeds and different systems of management. The main types associated with the lowlands are Down breeds and Longwools, which have a generally sturdy, almost square build with straight haunches. Most breeds are named after an area from which they presumably originated, such as the Suffolk, Oxford and Hampshire Down, or the Border Leicester and the Texel from Holland. Individual identification becomes complicated, however, as most commercial flocks are cross-bred in order to benefit from the best characteristics of the different types. Sometimes a particular feature will still be evident, such as the black face of the Suffolk or the prominent nose and forehead of the Border Leicester. Another confusion can arise when in winter one might see a flock of hill sheep grazing on some lowland pasture. This follows an old but now less common tradition of agistment when the flock would be brought down off the moors or mountains from quite another part of the country in order to escape the rigours of their native winter climate. It is now also not uncommon for special breeds to be

4 LIVESTOCK

kept, perhaps largely as a hobby, ranging from the now familiar Jacobs to tough Hebridean breeds.

In lowland areas sheep are likely to be kept only as part of a mixed farming enterprise, either in order to make use of some pasture land that is unsuited to arable cultivation or in conjunction with another livestock business such as horses or cattle. If the land is of an arable quality, it may be considered too valuable to be given over to the relatively modest returns that are gained from sheep. Where, however, this may be interspersed with grassland such as on the steep sides of the Downs then there will be reason to utilise that part of the farm with grazing for sheep or possibly cattle. Sheep are very efficient grazers and also quite nimble, so they can make good use of rough grass on steep slopes and can also follow behind larger animals such as cows or horses whose feeding patterns are such that they will leave grass behind them. Their droppings are also particularly beneficial in increasing the fertility of the land. In the hills, where the land is of a lesser potential, sheep form a larger and even exclusive role in the farm business, as mentioned in Chapter 5.

Financially, sheep enterprises depend now on just two factors: the sale of lambs and the receipt of subsidies. Previously, there would have also been a viable market for wool and for mutton. The fleece has to be sheared each year, if only to safeguard the health of the sheep, but it has in recent times fetched only negligible prices, due to poor skin values and a declining market for woollen products and to the availability of cheaper imports. Most wool produced in the UK is in fact used in carpet making rather than clothing, which requires a finer wool that tends to come from overseas. Some British wool is, however, exported, particularly to China, and the skins are sold worldwide. The ewes are retained for as long as they can breed successfully, which is usually for as long as they can eat adequately! The age of a sheep is often reckoned by the number of teeth that she has, building up to a total of eight (on the lower jaw only) in about the fourth year. Thereafter, depending on circumstances, these teeth begin to get broken or lost and this affects the ability to graze closely or under hard conditions. These 'broken-mouthed' ewes are either sold on to farms where feeding is made easier with, for example, the use of hay, or, more generally, they are culled and destined for the meat processing trade or for export. Mutton, or meat from older sheep, is still very occasionally butchered from a 'wether' or castrated ram that is over a year old, but the main market is now almost exclusively for lamb.

The fully grown sheep seen out in the pastures will therefore almost always be ewes aged between one and about five years old. The rams are much fewer in number, as mentioned below, and are likely to be kept separately in a small paddock until they are mated with the ewes, which is generally in the autumn. Sheep do not show their age particularly, although they do have a tendency to start limping which might make them appear rather old and arthritic. This is, however, likely to be just a case of foot rot, which is usually easily remedied by cleaning and medication, but which meanwhile can literally bring a sheep to its knees as it continues in search of fresh grazing.

Sheep are vulnerable to infections and infestations, so much so that many shepherds claim that they are all born with only one instinct and that is to die! Even after the old fleece has been shorn, the sheep is still liable to attack by parasites that can cause a number of ailments, notably sheep scab, mange or maggot infestation. One traditional method of preventing such infestations is to dip the sheep, which is a process that can still be seen (and smelt!) in the summer. The flock are all gathered in and passed through a specially constructed trough or bath in which they are immersed in a chemical solution. It used to be compulsory for all sheep to be dipped at least once a year, but there has recently been some uncertainty about whether the main agent, an organo-phosphate, could be sufficiently safely handled in this way. Some alternatives, such as giving injections or spraying the backs of the animals have been used instead, but dipping is still widely seen, albeit with the farmers or shepherds now protected with waterproofing and masks.

4 LIVESTOCK

Sheep's milk is now being produced commercially by a few specialist flocks, partly for cheese production and partly in liquid form for people who are allergic to cows' milk. This is, however, on a very limited scale and not making any particular visual impact on the landscape other than possibly a hoarding by a farm gate advertising sheep's milk for sale.

Like cattle, sheep also carry ear tags for identification and, indeed, it would be difficult even for the most diligent shepherd to tell them all apart. To most of us they would all look much alike, and it is remarkable to see how ewes and lambs recognise each other, by sound and smell, even in the hubbub of a large flock on the move.

Lambs

Sheep tend to be outside throughout the year, although it is becoming increasingly common for the ewes to be brought under cover for lambing. This not only improves the welfare of both ewe and lamb but also reduces the stress for the shepherd although it does require a high degree of management. In addition, it can allow for the lambs to be born earlier in the season and give protection against bad weather. Lambing may traditionally be a symbol of springtime but there is a premium price to be gained for the first of the year's lamb to be sold. With the advantage of scientific advances and of being able to shelter the animals against winter weather, there is an opportunity to have lambs born as early as Christmas time or even before and be ready to be sold for the Easter market. These early lambs may be kept under cover for the first few weeks, but can then be seen out of doors by February, depending upon the weather, and will need to be 'finished' within about four months from birth if they are to get the best price. In some cases, these early lambs are weaned at about three weeks and then provided with concentrate feeds.

During the winter, sheep are able to continue grazing, usually on grass whilst receiving a supplement of hay or cereal compounds and minerals, or sometimes on a root crop such as swedes or kale or on turnips that have

4 LIVESTOCK

been undersown into a cereal crop and are growing among the stubble after harvest. Depending on breed and circumstance, a lowland ewe may well have twin lambs and occasionally triplets, and the productivity of the flock is measured in terms of the percentage of lambs produced by the ewes together. In the lowlands, this tends to be between about 150% and 180%, although some do achieve more. The ewes are carefully managed before and during their pregnancy in order to achieve maximum fertility, especially by means of controlled feeding. The final average is easily reduced by the loss of some lambs that inevitably die, despite every effort taken to save each one. Many a lamb has survived into this world only after having been resuscitated in the bottom oven of an Aga or hand-fed with the aid of a pen filler! From there, those that were orphaned may progress to a 'lamb bar' or automatic milk dispenser or otherwise be adopted by a surrogate mother. When a ewe has triplets which all survive, one will have to be fostered out to another ewe who may have lost her only lamb or is able to take on a second. This again needs patience and skill on the part of the shepherd if the ewe is to accept the stranger; the shepherd often has to resort to a traditional subterfuge of clothing it in the skin of the dead lamb to make the ewe think that it is her own.

Once out in the field, some lambs can look a little smudged and bedraggled or as if they have been bleeding. This has probably been caused by a paint marker that has been applied on the back of the neck, either as an indication that some preventative injection or other treatment has been administered or to mark it with a number which corresponds to one that has been sprayed onto the mother.

In lowland flocks, the young lambs appear to have tails, whilst the older sheep do not. The lambs' tails are in fact removed at an early age by a painless process whereby the tail is constricted with a rubber ring so that it fails to grow and soon falls off. This is because on the richer diet of lowland pastures the tail is likely to become mucky and attract flies and disease. On the hills, where the grass is more sparse and where there may be fewer flies, this is less of a problem and the tail furthermore provides protection to the private (and rather important!) parts of the sheep against the cold mountain weather.

The female lambs, or 'gimmers' or 'ewe lambs' will often be retained in the flock at the end of the year, provided that they are of good enough quality to replace the older ewes in the following autumn. In some cases, ewe lambs are bred to be sold on to other flocks, or otherwise they tend to be sold with the ram lambs for slaughter. Some males may be kept over winter as 'store' lambs, either on their original farm or having been sold to another, and then slaughtered early in the following year at a heavier weight and a higher price than that which might have been obtained during the autumn glut. During winter, these stores will be grazed on forage crops such as kale, swede or stubble turnips. Unless being sold at the earliest markets, male lambs will have been castrated within a few days of being born and are then referred to as 'wethers'. This is to avoid the meat becoming tainted and also to avoid problems when out with the ewes and gimmers!

Rams

The ram, or rams, will run with the ewes in the open field in the autumn or early winter according to when lambing is to take place. Although it might be expected that they would be distinguished from the ewes by sporting a macho pair of horns, this is now rare and one will normally have to look at the underside of the rear of the animal rather than the top front in order to spot the difference! Another indicator may be a rather undignified harness that is worn by the ram during the mating period and on which is strapped a block of a marking agent or 'raddle'. This rubs off each time he mounts a ewe leaving a splash of colour on her back to signal to the shepherd that the deed has been done! Depending on his age and prowess and how widely the flock is ranged, a ram is expected to service or 'tup' around 50 ewes.

4 LIVESTOCK

Although not thought of in the same way as bulls, rams can also be aggressive and difficult to handle.

Pigs

Pigs have become more evident again in the landscape in recent years, as they are now kept increasingly out of doors with distinctive semi-circular shelters or 'arks'. These pigs are generally the sows and young females or 'gilts' who are either pregnant or due to be mated. They forage heavily in the field, which soon becomes very muddy and mucky, but they do not depend on grass for grazing as they are fed daily with a cereal-based feed.

When the sows are due to give birth or 'farrow', they are moved inside where the piglets can be better protected. The young pigs are then usually kept in fattening pens or yards under a controlled climate and with a carefully managed feeding regime. There are occasions when the piglets are kept out in the open with the sows, but they are then more difficult to manage and vulnerable to fighting, predators and adverse weather. Pigs are surprisingly sensitive to weather conditions, especially hot sun, against which they require shade or, as can often be seen, a pool of water in which to wallow.

4 LIVESTOCK

Pig buildings themselves are not always particularly visible, as they are of a low construction and often in relatively isolated positions. Their low height is for reasons of economy and the need to be able to maintain the necessary range of temperatures, but beside each building there is often a tall feed silo. Their isolation is in order to minimise the risk of disease to which pig herds can be very vulnerable, especially when kept in such close and controlled environments. Most pig units operate rigorous precautions to prevent the spread of any infections and tend to limit the amount of direct contact from outside, even to the extent of requiring anyone going onto the property to drive or walk through a bath of disinfectant. This will explain the seemingly unfriendly notices that are often posted around asking people not to enter the land; it is not simply a case of farmers being possessive and unwelcoming, but a necessary measure to prevent potential disaster from striking the herd. Also, although pigs are far more hygienic by nature than their reputation would suggest, they do create a strong smell and this is another reason why their sheds may be sited out of the public eye, or nose!

Whilst in years gone by most farms would have had their own pigs, the commercial herds have latterly been concentrated around the arable areas of eastern Britain. This is partly because the muck can then be disposed of onto the arable fields, and partly due to the ready availability of barley and other cereals that comprise the pigs' diet and provide the straw that is used in some housing systems. These eastern arable areas happen also to be close to the North Sea ports and are convenient therefore for the importation of cheaper feedstuffs. This explains why there are pig units concentrated in locations such as in Humberside, near to Hull.

The older traditional types of pigs are now confined mostly to small herds that specialise in rare breeds and the bigger commercial ones have a more universal appearance, using newer hybrid strains which all look rather alike. These are based originally on one or two of the old breeds, such as the Landrace and the Large White, and occasionally also the Saddleback which still produces a distinctive band of white behind the front shoulders.

Artificial insemination is used widely, but many herds will also have their own boars, although they are generally kept in yards or pens and are not therefore seen out and about. These modern developments have resulted in ever improving performance and a sow can now produce a litter of about ten piglets every five months. This rather rapid turnover can provide the level of performance needed to produce pork at acceptable prices, but it is does make the industry vulnerable to the changing fortunes of the 'pig cycle' and to the ensuing unstable incomes, as well as to concerns about animal welfare. Pigs may look rather endearing, but sows can be very aggressive to each other, causing injuries and poor feeding. In fact, until only recently, they would often have been tethered in stalls to keep them from fighting and to ensure that each received a proper measure of feed. This has now been banned in the UK and the use of arks and free-ranging systems has become more evident as a result, together with less intensive covered yards. Breeding sows tend to be kept in the herd for about six litters or approximately three years.

Poultry

Chickens

As with pigs, there are now more chickens to be seen in the countryside than previously, when almost all commercial flocks would have been housed indoors. Those that may be seen out of doors are laying hens that are producing free range eggs. The rearing of chickens for meat, or 'broilers', is still confined within buildings, as is the production of eggs for breeding. The bulk of commercial egg production is also still done inside, using 'batteries' or, to a lesser extent, in open planned barns.

The more extensive system of free range egg production comes as a response to one sector of the market that not only prefers a more natural food source, but is also prepared to pay a premium price to cover the greater costs involved. Free range may sound like a natural process but it

4 LIVESTOCK

is nonetheless rigorously defined by the European regulations in terms of the amount of space available to each hen. The hens do in fact roost and lay within a shed, where they are also fed, whilst having access during daylight hours to surrounding grassland. In the alternative system where the hens are confined in batteries or cages, there are greater efficiencies in the conversion of feed and the control of disease as well as greater economies of scale so that the eggs can be produced more cheaply. Not only can energy levels and food intake be monitored more accurately in a battery house, but the light can be controlled artificially so as to extend the hen's working day!

Keeping hens in battery cages sounds rather uncivilised and is certainly a controversial concept. It is, however, an extremely efficient system that has provided a reliable supply of eggs at low cost over many years. For the birds to be fully productive, they have to be in good condition and for that they need to be kept in the best possible environment. In that respect, battery houses provide all that is required for the hens' welfare. However, the thought that they are so closely confined and literally caged in, gives rise to concern. These issues are coming under increasing European regulation, with the raising of minimum acceptable standards especially with regard to the size of cages and the numbers accommodated within them. Interestingly, past experiments to make the cages less harsh by installing a softer or solid floor failed as the hens preferred to stand on a mesh base which was more like the natural roosts for which their feet have evolved.

Barn eggs come from hens that are confined indoors but are free to roam within a large building. There is also a premium market for these eggs, as with free range production, but it has been a less successful concept. Within the barn the birds roam on a floor covered in a 'deep litter' of wood shavings or similar material and then have access to laying boxes and roosts around the building. Whilst giving a little more natural movement to the hens than those in battery cages, it is a more difficult system to manage and can lead to losses of both eggs and birds.

4 LIVESTOCK

Battery houses and broiler sheds are, as with pig houses, often unobtrusive in that they are positioned in isolated sites and of low construction, silhouetted only by a feed silo. As with pigs, disease is a constant concern and every effort is made to protect the birds from infections that can spread with such devastating effect through flocks in such close confinement.

Broilers bred for eating are reared from chicks in big barns in which they have freedom to move across a floor that has a suitable bedding or 'litter'. The efficiency of the system is such that it takes only seven or eight weeks for the birds to grow to the desired weight and configuration required by the poultry market. It may not quite be the image of a clutch of chickens pecking freely around a farmyard, but it is thanks to the broiler industry that chicken has been transformed from being a treat affordable only on a Sunday just a generation ago to the popular and palatable food that it has become today.

Hens' eggs can have either white or brown shells and the latter is generally considered more attractive and somehow more healthy too. This is in fact determined by the particular breed of the laying birds and is not an indication of their diet or living conditions. The colour of the yolks can, however, be enhanced by changing the balance of ingredients in the feed.

Turkeys
Turkey meat production has increased substantially over recent years, having grown from a home-spun seasonal exercise to an all-year-round

international industry. On individual farms, birds can still be seen being fattened in barns or yards for the Christmas market. Elsewhere, the commercial turkey sheds look very similar to the broiler houses mentioned above and are also often quite unobtrusive, as the flocks are equally prone to infectious diseases.

Ducks and Geese

Geese are still largely produced just as a sideline on a seasonal basis and have not been exploited by the major food processing interests. Ducks are produced in a similar, but as yet smaller, commercial environment to that of broilers and turkeys. They can also occasionally be seen foraging on a free range system out of doors, but such flocks are still rather specialised and rarely seen.

Horses

From the Middle Ages through to the outbreak of the Second World War horses were an essential part of the farmland scene. Even in 1939 there were still 12 times as many working horses in Britain as there were tractors. Twenty years later the number of horses had dwindled to only one fifth of the total of tractors. Now horses are kept solely for recreational purposes, but do nonetheless make a noticeable impact on some areas of the country. One such sign is that of training jumps which have sometimes been set up in a paddock. Since part of their purpose is to replicate eventing courses, they are often made out of colourfully painted materials such as wooden bars or old oil drums or traffic bollards, which tend to stand out in an otherwise rural setting. Another sign is the white tape that sometimes runs along the top of fences around the fields, which is less likely to cause injury to horses than razor wire and is a more visible barrier.

Horse riding is a popular pastime that appeals to a wide cross-section of people, many of whom do not have land upon which they can keep their steeds. As a consequence, in certain areas farmers have increasingly converted their buildings to stables and given over paddocks for horse grazing, especially where they are close to a centre of population or in a holiday location. In other situations, this may be for the more commercial purpose of training racehorses, with large and well maintained yards and with paddocks divided by post and rail fences. These establishments depend upon being able to exercise their horse on as many days in the year as possible and this in turn depends on the land around them. That land needs to be open, reasonably remote and, above all, free-draining and free of frost. It will often also incorporate sloping ground which is useful for developing the horses' muscles. These conditions are found, for example, in the limestone of soils of the Berkshire Downs or the sands of Newmarket Heath and it is for this reason that one will see there long stretches of marked out and mown grass that form the 'gallops'.

Ponies, which is the description given to the smaller breed of horses, are found in three main contexts: at riding schools and livery stables; when used for trekking; and in areas such as Dartmoor and the New Forest in Hampshire. In these particular locations, the ponies can be seen roaming free across the large area that makes up the moor or forest. Whilst this may give the impression that they are wild herds, the majority are in fact individually owned and are indeed often reared for commercial purposes. Pony trekking takes place mostly in the upland areas of Britain, where there can also be ponies in the wild, as mentioned again in that context in Chapter 5.

Exotics

There is an increasing diversity of livestock being reared in Britain, ranging from alpacas to ostriches and even worm farming! These ventures are still of a rather specialised nature and it is rare therefore to see such animals out on the land. Many of them have been introduced on the basis that they

produce a lean and allegedly healthy meat that has generally been grown in free range conditions. Some, like the alpaca, may have a particularly fine and therefore valuable fleece. Others might be bred for the purpose of being sold on as pets, as in the case of pigmy ponies or pot-bellied pigs.

Deer farming is perhaps more commonly seen and can be distinguished by the fact the pastures will be enclosed by specially high fences. Goats are now also not unusual, with an increasing demand for their milk from those who suffer allergies against dairy products, as well as a growing fashion for goats cheese.

Rare Breeds

As with some of the exotic animals, flocks or herds of the rarer breeds of British farm stock are not seen particularly often in the countryside, although there is a certain amount of evidence of them. They may well form part of an attraction at a farm visitor centre or be offered in the shops as a special quality of organic meat. It has already been mentioned at the beginning of this chapter how much more diverse dairy herds used to be in this country and how they now all tend to be of just one or other commercial breed. The same has occurred in most of the other livestock sectors, so that many of the traditional strains of farm animals were discarded in favour of more productive modern cross-breeds. In more recent times, efforts have been made by enthusiasts and the breed societies to ensure that the older varieties do not become extinct and that some of the original breeds are preserved. As a result, many of them have now been re-introduced, generally on a relatively small scale, but often in situations where they may be seen by the public. Whilst some of these breeds do produce a meat that can command a select premium market, they are unlikely ever to compete on more general terms with the ever-improving commercial performance of the modern varieties.

Dorset Horn sheep

4 LIVESTOCK

Fish Farming

Fish farms are of a rather specialised nature but they have become increasingly noticeable in the countryside, if only because they need to be in an accessible location and most of them depend on retail trade and therefore have to advertise themselves.

Fish farms are predominantly for trout, or occasionally for ornamental carp, and need a particular source of water which therefore limits them to certain areas of the country. Trout flourish in clear chalky streams and the farmed variety (predominantly the rainbow trout) is bred in pools or open tanks that are formed off such streams. The process of rearing them has become highly technical and intensive, even though it uses some basic principles that originated in the days of the medieval monasteries. With the large number of fish being produced on a modern farm, disease and pollution are a constant threat and have to be carefully controlled.

Trout can also be reared in large cages in lakes, as opposed to tanks or pools fed by a running stream, although this is still rare. Such cages can be seen, too, moored off the sea shore, where they are most likely to be for salmon and occasionally trout or sometimes now on an experimental basis for white fish. The salmon farms are restricted to areas where the fish has a natural habitat in the wild, predominantly around Scotland.

Organic Livestock

There is no visible means of telling whether livestock out in the fields is being produced by organic methods or not. Perhaps the fact that some of these are outside at all is a sign that they might be organic, since intensive indoor production is usually incompatible with organic principles, although of course many non-organic animals are grazed out in the open too. Organic farming is referred to again in Chapter 11, but in this context it

4 LIVESTOCK

could be summarised as being a production method that avoids the use of artificial ingredients. This relates not only to the land on which the animals forage, but also to the additional feed that they may be given, especially in winter, and to any medication that they receive. As with arable farming, this will involve skilled and intensive management in order to produce competitive returns and it tends also to result in lower yields. This is due to such factors as lesser levels of fertiliser, less concentrated feedstuffs and a preference for avoiding the use of certain medication such as antibiotics to combat injury or illness. With organic livestock there is, however, an additional factor not considered in arable farming, namely that of animal welfare. It is automatically implied that when stock has been reared organically it will have enjoyed the highest welfare standards. This will have a special appeal to consumers even though it is probable that similar standards are being maintained on other farms too. It is possible for just part of a farm to be certified as organic so that, for example, the livestock might be reared in accordance with organic principles while the arable land is still being run on conventional lines.

Buildings

Mention has already been made in the preceding sections about some of the buildings to be found in connection with livestock rearing and it is not really feasible or appropriate to give any more detailed description of them. The purpose of this section is to point out the general features by which the type of farm can be recognised and the kind of enterprises that are being run there. In general it could be said that, although it may seem unnatural to enclose farm animals within buildings, the farmer's main purpose is to ensure that the beasts thrive and are in good condition. Great care is therefore taken to ensure that the design of the buildings and the way in which they are used provide an environment in which this can be achieved.

4 LIVESTOCK

Dairying

Although cows use one particular building every day of the year, it is a relatively small one and one will tend to notice first the various areas that are really only occupied during the winter. The daily activity is of course milking (in fact two or three times daily, as already mentioned). This is carried out in what goes by the rather charming-sounding description of the milking parlour. Images of milk maids with pails and churns are far from the modern reality, however, as the parlour is built around a double row of steel stalls and buzzes to the sound of a compressor that works the milking machines and, as often as not, pop music from a radio! (Whether cows produce better yields when hearing music is not as yet proven but it certainly helps the herdsmen cope with being faced with lines of cows' hindquarters for two or three hours.) The cows are let in through a sliding door and walk into the stalls, making a herringbone shape on either side of a central pit. They learn to stand facing the outer walls so that their udders are conveniently within reach of the herdsmen, although in many systems they have an encouragement to do so in that there is a line of individual feeding troughs along the outer wall. These troughs are filled with a supplementary feed, while from the central pit each cow is attached to the milking lines by a cluster of suction teats that fit onto their udders. The number of cows being milked at any one time depends upon the size of the installation, but the cows may well be in two rows of 10 or 20 being looked after by one or two personnel according to the degree of automation in the feeding mechanism and in the removal of the clusters.

Once all of the cows have been milked, a door is opened at the far end of the stalls and they walk out to leave space for the next batch to come in. The cows enter from a collecting yard, which can be either covered or open and tends to be circular, as this allows for the animals to be brought forward in an orderly fashion, being pushed gently when necessary by a centrally pivoted sprung gate. Despite the likelihood of the cows bringing muck and mud into the parlour, high standards of hygiene have to be maintained. The cows' udders are washed down before milking and all surfaces and equipment are of course kept clean throughout. The milk is then piped into an adjacent room which is still referred to as the dairy but which nowadays contains just a very clinical-looking stainless steel tank. The milk is cooled down in this tank and held there until collection by road tanker within one or now possibly two days.

In winter, the morning milking starts before dawn and the evening session finishes after dusk, so that the yards and the parlour buildings are often lit up, providing a strange contrast to the extensive darkness of a country night. A few of the largest dairy farms have rotary parlours in which the milking stalls are mounted on a large circular platform that revolves around the herdsmen who work standing in a shallow pit in the centre as if in the hub of a wheel. A further innovation that is still very new and unusual is a robotic parlour whereby cows bring themselves into a stall and are automatically attached to the clusters and the hydraulic milking line. The herdsman's main task is then to watch a computer screen rather than handle the stock.

Rotary parlour

In some farmyards, one may still see a low range of buildings constructed of brick or concrete block under a slate or tiled roof and lit with old-fashioned windows rather than transparent sheets within the roof. These would be the former cowsheds in which the cows would have been lined up in parallel stalls to be milked individually or, in more recent times, by machine. Such buildings became too inefficient and labour intensive and have been replaced by parlours, with some being adapted for calf housing.

Outside, the more noticeable structures will include covered yards or cubicle buildings in which the cows spend the winter, and possibly a silage clamp and slurry tank. There are also usually open-sided Dutch barns for the storage of hay and straw and an implement shed and workshop. The covered yard is a portal-framed building partly enclosed with block walling and partly faced with ventilated boards known as 'Yorkshire boarding' or netting. The floor is covered with straw and the whole area is used for bedding as well as for a general living area. The building may also have feeding troughs depending on whether the cows eat direct from the clamp or have the silage or other feed brought to them. Alternatively, the yard may be fitted with lines of cubicles that are like individual stalls of wood or steel backing on to a central dunging area. This cubicle arrangement can sometimes be fitted into a lower type of building known as cow kennels in which the stalls back onto a central open passage and are generally built of timber. On many occasions, however, these cubicles might be fitted inside a covered yard and consequently might not be distinguishable from outside. The cows need less bedding material in this system and the manure is therefore less bulky and can be scraped out regularly as slurry and held in tanks or lagoons. Some designs even have slatted floors so that the slurry can be drained away from the building automatically.

Slurry handling is a major issue in dairy farming. Slurry is destined ultimately to be spread onto the land as fertiliser, but this can often only take place after the winter when the ground is dry enough. It has meanwhile to be stored in safety and in all weathers, either in earth-sided lagoons or in steel tanks. In covered yards where straw is used on the floor it is replenished regularly and then may only be cleared out once when the cows have gone out again in the spring, by which time the land should be dry enough to allow the muck spreading to take place.

Dairy calves and followers are housed in similar yards or open-fronted buildings and are generally bedded on straw as well. Young calves reared on milk substitutes are kept in smaller pens, either within a larger yard or in a former cowshed or stable block. Alongside most dairy or beef units, there will also be storage for hay and straw in 'Dutch barns' that comprise tall, open-sided sheds constructed generally of steel stanchions and corrugated roof sheeting.

Slurry handling

There is a new system of management that may now be seen on a few farms where the cattle are kept in an open yard throughout the winter. This yard is laid with a suitable material such as wood chippings that will drain off and remain reasonably clean, and the cows seem able to thrive without cover provided that they are fed well. Another innovation that may be seen occasionally is the use of calf hutches in which young calves are accommodated in individual units looking rather like a modernised plastic dog kennel!

Beef Cattle

Beef cattle are housed in covered yards or open-fronted sheds similar to those on a dairy farm and which may even have been used previously for a dairy herd. The cattle do not use the cubicle system and tend to be bedded on straw. A beef herd may well be run together with another farm enterprise, as mentioned previously, and the buildings could then form part of a larger yard with, say, crop stores. Beef cattle are more likely to have feed brought to mangers in the yard than be allowed to self-feed on silage. There will then have to be covered storage either for straw that has been treated with a suitable additive or for cereal compounds. Some beef units have slatted floors which require no bedding as the slurry drains away through channels beneath the floor rather than being mulched into the straw, as with the more traditional systems. In all cases, as with the covered yards for dairy cows, ample ventilation has to be provided through Yorkshire boarding or plastic netting or roof ducts.

Sheep

In the lowlands, sheep are likely to be brought inside only at lambing time, or in the period just before lambing. This takes place in a covered yard or smaller shed that will be protected with cladding or ventilated netting. There is little that is distinctive about such buildings when seen from a distance, and often it will be an existing corn store or implement shed that is adapted temporarily for the purpose. Lambs do, however, get born around the clock and there will therefore be lights on at night. There will also probably be some electric heaters available for those lambs which need

some initial support, although the building overall will need to be ventilated at all times, even at times of cold temperatures because otherwise the ewes could become liable to respiratory and other diseases.

Pigs and Poultry

Reference has already been made to the buildings used for intensive pig and poultry production. They are significantly lower than the covered yards in dairy or beef enterprises and are often constructed of timber. They do have a slightly sinister appearance in that in place of windows they have a series of enclosed vents looking like inverted hoppers. Also, unlike a cattle yard, there is no sight or sound of the stock and the surrounding areas are scrupulously clean and tidy, even to the point of appearing quite lifeless. This is all in aid of protecting the stock from disease and providing them with a constant environment. Feed tends to be stored in vertical silos beside each building, which often stand out against the skyline above the long low structures of the animal housing. Once again, especially for battery houses, it is likely that lights will be on in the winter after dark.

Horses

The full equestrian establishment will be easily recognisable, with ranges of loose boxes and Dutch barns for the storage of hay and straw, although more sophisticated and less bulky forms of bedding are now often used instead. On farms, these boxes may well have been converted from old calf pens or piggeries and be facing into what would have been the traditional yard. It is not uncommon also to see a training area, or 'manege', either as an open area with an all-weather material on the ground or as a portal-framed building covering a rather wider span than the usual agricultural yard. Another tell-tale sign of an equestrian enterprise is the sight of the horse box lorries that are sometimes too tall to be garaged within a building and will be standing out in the open yard.

4 LIVESTOCK

Transport

Sometimes, farm stock can attract as much attention on the public roads as out in the fields. A large truck with slatted sides through which one can see, hear and perhaps even smell a mass of sheep or pigs is rather more noticeable than a closed container lorry carrying some anonymous and inanimate load. Horse boxes, too, become rather evident as they seem to travel so slowly, often on narrow lanes with few places in which to pass!

Transporting animals can be an emotive subject, especially when they appear to be in such cramped and unnatural conditions. There are, however, now extensive welfare regulations governing such transport and it is in the interests of all involved that the animals do not suffer during their journey. These journeys will tend to be to a market or abattoir or from one farm to another. In most cases they are over relatively short distances, although the cost of implementing increasingly stringent health and welfare requirements in abattoirs and markets has caused many of the smaller local businesses to close. As a result, animals do now often have to travel further than before. However, when going to a market, the farmer will be keen that his stock are presented there in good condition so as to attract the best possible price. It is worth ensuring that they do not arrive off the lorry in a mucky or injured state. Even when being taken to an abattoir it is important to avoid the stock being badly treated, as this causes stress which in turn creates adrenaline within the animals and has a surprisingly damaging effect on the meat. To a person looking in through the slats of a cattle truck, it may seem that the animals are overcrowded and certainly it is economical to take the maximum number in each load. However, the fact that the animals are sandwiched in (rather like commuters in a London underground train in rush hour) means that they support each other and are less likely to sway about with the movement of the lorry or fall over during the journey. Horses, on the other hand, are transported individually or in separate stalls and there is less protection therefore against such movement. As a result, the vehicles will travel more slowly and with seemingly exaggerated care around corners or over humps.

5 THE UPLANDS

older, more woody, growth and allows new shoots to develop and to provide a better habitat and feeding ground for the all-important grouse.

Fencing is a significant feature throughout most of the uplands as sheep and cattle are so predominant, except on the highest ground where the landscape is too wild for them to be feasibly contained. Such fences are of post and wire but can also still be in the form of old drystone walls that predate the availability of galvanised wire. Even the woodland plantations need to be fenced off when newly established, as sheep would otherwise browse on the leading shoots of the young trees. In some areas such fencing may be extended in height so as to protect the trees additionally from being damaged by deer, which will also graze on the tops or strip off new bark. Much of the upland pasture does not have any roadside fences as the distances over which they would have to be constructed would be economically unviable in relation to the amount of traffic that uses those roads. Instead, the livestock are retained within their territory by cattle grids placed at either end.

Tourism may be an important part of the upland economy but it produces little direct return from the land itself, as access to unfenced land is free to those who wish to enjoy it. It can, however, involve some management costs in the provision of signposts, gates or stiles or of parking areas. The income from tourism comes more from the provision of services such as accommodation, refreshments and shops rather than from the land.

The subsidies that are specifically targeted at the uplands and which are outlined in Chapter 9 have little visible impact upon the landscape itself other than simply that the land is still being farmed. The net income derived from sheep and beef has fallen so much in real terms that few, if any, farmers would have been able to continue running their holdings without the extra payments made through the subsidies. It is feared that the current changes in this support system will result in more hill farmers having to face unsustainable losses, with payments being made on an area rather then headage basis and linked increasingly to environmental conditions. There are some grants that are made specifically towards the provision of items that can be seen out in the open rather than be identified only in a farmer's bank statement. These might be for the provision of public access or larger local developments, such as a windfarm or hydroelectric scheme.

Forestry and field sports, the other two main planks of the upland economy, both involve active land management which can sometimes be seen as it takes place, especially in the case of thinning a forestry plantation. These two topics are dealt with separately in Chapters 6 and 8.

Sheep

When all is said and done, sheep have always been the mainstay of the uplands and indeed in most districts they will vastly outnumber humans! Hill sheep are a different proposition to the lowland flocks described in Chapter 4. In the uplands they are likely to form the essential core of the farm business, rather than a complementary part of a mixed enterprise. The flocks are larger in number and grazed over a far wider area, often covering many hundreds of hectares. Pastures tend furthermore to be on steep ground with a rather inhospitable climate and produce only poor grazing. The sheep (and their shepherds!) need therefore to be of hardy stock and able to thrive under such discouraging conditions. They tend to be of a different type to their lowland counterparts, although the two are now often cross-bred with the purpose of introducing a better performance whilst still preserving the necessary hardiness. Traditionally, the hill breeds have a less bulky frame and longer and more nimble legs, a longer and looser looking fleece and will have retained their tails (in contrast to the lowland practice of docking mentioned in Chapter 4). Many of them are named after the area from which the breed must have originated or been

5 THE UPLANDS

most commonly used, such as the Herdwick, Swaledale and Cheviot. (Strictly speaking, sheep are subdivided further into distinct hill and upland breeds so that, for example, the Clun from Shropshire is in the upland category rather than being a hill sheep such as the Welsh Mountain, although their home pastures may not be all that far apart in miles or in height above sea level.) Another rather strange nomenclature arises from the crossing of hill and down sheep to produce a popular type know as mules, which have nothing whatever to do with horses or asses!

In winter, the flocks are brought down off the highest ground to pastures that are more sheltered and closer to the farmstead where they can be better tended and provided with supplementary feed. Traditionally, some would even be taken further down to lowland farms, as mentioned in Chapter 4. Lambing, which occurs generally in April and May and much later than on many lowland farms, will also take place on this lower or 'in-bye' land or within the farmyard itself. In summer, the flocks move up onto the hills and are left to graze. Where the terrain is difficult and the grass relatively poor, each sheep will need a much greater area in which to graze than when on more fertile pastures, so that sometimes there will be on average only about two or three ewes per hectare. A normal flock of a few hundred sheep will therefore cover a considerable expanse of moor and mountain and will be far harder to manage than when enclosed in some lowland meadow.

Traditionally, such flocks are controlled by sheep dogs and one can often see from afar the extraordinary flow of white marks that are the sheep being rounded up and directed by a pair of black and white collies. The only modern concession that might be noticed is that the shepherds (or flockmasters as they are now often called) are working with them from an all-terrain quadbike rather than on foot or with a pony. Some flocks even manage themselves to a degree, in that the sheep know their territory through being hefted (brought up for generations on the same hillside) and therefore have the instinct to remain on it or at least to return to it at some stage. Even so, hill sheep do get lost or mixed up between neighbours and they tend therefore to be marked by a distinctive notch put into the edge of their ears or with a large paint mark or brand, so that they can be recognised from a distance as belonging to a particular farmer. Whilst out grazing on the hill, sheep do often live up to their name by following each other in a strict single line, so much so that they often wear down a very visible path. These sheep tracks can be seen from a distance and may look as if they are proper paths, although in fact they represent a right of way for sheep rather than humans!

From time to time, the flocks have to be gathered in. As in the lowlands, they will need to be shorn or dipped, but in the hills they may also have to be counted for the purpose of claiming subsidy, which can be a major exercise involving both man and dog. In contrast to the lowlands where there is every advantage in ewes producing twins, in the hills ewes are likely to be accompanied by just a single lamb as the conditions are less able to provide the extra sustenance needed for both the ewe and each of the twin lambs.

Cattle

Devon cattle

The pasture in the hills would be too poor and the situation too remote to sustain any modern commercial dairy production, but the lower slopes may well support beef cattle in the form of a suckler herd, as described in the lowland context in Chapter 4. As with sheep, there are some breeds of cattle that derive from the hill areas, such as the Welsh Black, the Luing or the shaggy coated Highland, but, in the main, even in the uplands the suckler herds will now often be a commercial cross of different strains of cattle. As with sheep, cattle in the uplands will tend to raise just one calf since the conditions would not readily support multiple suckling as is practised in the lowlands. Although hardy by nature, these cattle herds are likely to be housed in covered yards throughout the winter and fed on a diet of silage and cereal concentrates.

5 THE UPLANDS

Horses

Ponies can sometimes be seen grazing the hills and moors. In the more popular areas these may well be kept for pony trekking. In other locations that are near to former coal mining districts, these could be wild stock descended from former pit ponies that were released onto the hills once they had completed their working lives.

Buildings

On the higher slopes of the hills themselves, there will occasionally be signs of a former stone building that is now only a ruin but which would once have been a farmstead, cattle shelter or fodder store. Those farms that have survived to the present day tend to be on the lower slopes or in the valleys. Alongside the farmhouse, there may well still be a range of traditional stone buildings that have been retained over the years as they can still provide useful storage and accommodation. This is in contrast to arable enterprises where the increasing size of machinery and the trend towards specialisation has resulted in such buildings being replaced with modern structures. The hill farm is, however, likely also to have a Dutch barn for the storage of hay and straw and a covered yard to house the cattle and provide shelter for lambing.

Recreation

The hills are now frequently a place for recreation as well as for farming or forestry. Sometimes this is readily visible, as with the ski lifts in the Scottish mountains or the well-worn paths of the Lake District, although in most cases the impact is less dramatic. The signs are seen firstly in the farmsteads themselves rather than out on the land, with many of them offering accommodation and other facilities. Pony trekking is a further extension of

5 THE UPLANDS

this, giving rise to the sight of horses again in the countryside, whether being ridden out along the hill paths or just grazing in the meadows. Other activities take place on the land but without much involvement of the farmer or landowner, as people take to cross-country driving, biking or hand gliding. Field sports in the form of stalking or grouse shooting have few physical signs other than seeing the 'butts' or heather being burnt.

In the woods, the Forestry Commission has often responded to the demand for recreation by creating car parks and marked and maintained paths, which would have been most unusual at the time when most of them were first planted in what were then remote and unvisited hillsides. The influx of visitors into the upland areas has also led to the improvement of some of the original single track roads, sometimes with funding from the European Commission. Visitor centres and other holiday attractions are further developments that have taken place within the more accessible upland districts and are providing new uses for former farmyards.

Forestry

Forestry, which is so widely evident across the hills, is the subject of the next chapter.

107

6 WOODS AND FORESTS

General Background

At the time of the Norman Conquest most of Britain was thickly wooded, with either native forest trees or scrub or a mixture of the two. Over the intervening centuries much of this has been cleared, primarily to create the farmland and grazing needed to sustain a growing population and also, in some areas, to provide timber for ship building, other construction work and fuel. What now remains is a small vestige of these ancient woodlands and evidence, too, of a more modern attempt at replacing them. The original forests would have comprised mostly broadleaved trees, which are the familiar deciduous hardwoods such as oak, ash or beech. Over the years, conifers have been introduced, providing us with the largely evergreen softwoods including pine, spruces and fir.

The areas of old woods will have survived for a variety of reasons: because they stand on land that has always been unsuitable for farming; because they provide shelter, whether for a farmstead or for foxes and pheasants; or because they formed a traditional part of an estate's economic life or other amenity. Such situations are more likely to apply in those parts of the country where the land is of a poorer quality, or on hillsides or in an area of greater rainfall. In the fens of East Anglia, for example, where the topography and quality of land favour intensive arable production, there are fewer woods than in, say, Devon with its steep valleys that are difficult to cultivate and a wetter climate that is so much better suited to trees. On the other hand, there are areas also in the east where trees grow in abundance, notably around the Thetford Chase in Suffolk where, despite a dry climate and level land, there is a great expanse of forest due to the fact that the soils are too light for productive farming.

The modern replacements of our ancient woods are to be seen in the uplands in the form of serried ranks of conifer plantations. Although hardly equivalent to the old broadleaved woods, these plantations arose from a genuine desire to restore some of the nation's timber resource that had been

lost through the two World Wars. During the first of these in particular, coal was the essential source of power for manufacturing and for ships and the mines depended on timber pit props. The volume of timber that was taken for the war effort had depleted the country's stock of mature trees and these had to be replaced without delay. The traditional broadleaved forest trees such as oak or beech take over 100 years to mature and are not in fact particularly used for mining timber. Conifers, on the other hand, grow more rapidly and can produce pit props in half that time. Furthermore, these conifers would grow well on hills and moorland which had only restricted use for farming. On the other hand, for broadleaved trees to thrive they need to be on lower land, which would be likely to have agricultural potential too. As food production was also a strategic priority at the time, there was a double reason for selecting conifers as the most appropriate means for replenishing the national timber resources.

When these coniferous woods did reach maturity and were felled, there was a policy to replant them with similar varieties so that the effect upon the landscape was perpetuated. In later years, steps were taken to soften the impact of blocks of dark conifers by following the contour lines and avoiding rigid rectangular compartments or by mixing different species. More recently still, replanting policy in many of these areas requires the inclusion of some natural broadleaved species, such as silver birch, which have a lesser commercial potential but give the plantation a more varied and attractive appearance.

The Forestry Commission

Forestry is in fact still very closely regulated by government, through direct public ownership and by policy controls over private woodland. To achieve the aims of post-war policy in 1919, the Forestry Commission was established with the dual purpose of on the one hand acquiring existing woods or land for planting and on the other of administering policy and grant aid. Land was either purchased outright or leased off the freehold owners, often for a term of 999 years, which seems a very far-sighted position to have taken even for a slow-growing product such as timber that takes a relatively long time to mature! This was, however, a valid means by which the Commission could acquire woodlands that lay within private estates and this arrangement can still be seen today. With changing circumstances, some rationalisation was introduced around the 1980s with a programme of sales of woods owned by the Forestry Commission. This was, however, subsequently halted, due largely to the question of whether the free access allowed through public woods could be secured after they had been transferred to private ownership. The Commission does therefore still own as much as 800,000 hectares of woodland throughout Britain. Its jurisdiction covers all three devolved parts of the country, with policy and grant aid being administered by the Forestry Authority and the management of its own woods being run by Forestry Enterprise.

6 WOODS AND FORESTS

Felling Licences

Outside the Commission's own woods, forestry policy is enforced on private owners by means of licences and grants. It is illegal for anyone to cut down more than 5 cubic metres of timber per year without first obtaining a felling licence from the Forestry Authority. This means that anyone wishing to do more than remove just a single old tree or a small cluster of younger ones needs firstly to get official approval. Such approval is granted whenever there is good reason for this to be done, such as for normal forestry practice or because the trees have reached maturity. It is, however, almost always coupled with a requirement that the land must be replanted with new trees. Originally, this was to ensure that such trees as had been removed would be replaced, probably by the same or a similar species. More recently, though, a condition may be imposed that the new plantings include a different species, notably for broadleaved trees where conifers grew before. This is with the specific aim of bringing more native trees back into the landscape and of softening the impact made over the years by uniform coniferous planting.

New plantings approved by the Authority are then eligible for grant aid, as without such help it would be difficult to see how most woodland owners could meet the cost of establishing the young trees, with the danger that the ground would be left untended. The management process of starting, growing and felling a wood is described later in this chapter. Sometimes, a felling licence may require that a few of the old trees be left standing, even though this would not be normal forestry practice. Such a requirement would usually be in order to preserve something of the earlier skyline rather than create a completely flat area of land, or it may be as part of a policy of natural regeneration. However, not all such well-intentioned plans will succeed, as once trees are left standing without those that had grown around them, they become much more vulnerable to being blown over. Similarly, difficulties can arise with the policy of replanting solely with broadleaves since such trees tend to become better established when mixed in with conifers, despite the public preference for seeing more of the former. One imagines woods and forests to cover large areas and that any operation within them, such as felling, would make a vast scar upon the landscape. In fact, most woods, especially in the lowlands, are divided into relatively small compartments so that the work carried out within them is generally on a limited scale, as mentioned later.

Whilst felling licences are only required when what amounts to more than one or two trees are being cut down, there is also a means by which an owner might be restrained from removing even one individual tree. This would be through the application of a Tree Preservation Order which can be imposed by the local planning authority in cases where the tree, or a group of trees, has a particular visual or historic merit. All trees do of course have a finite lifespan that cannot be prolonged for ever, although there is a growing trend towards preserving some of them for as long as possible. It is possible, therefore, to see, particularly in parks and public places, examples of old gnarled trees, some of which have had to have dead or dangerous branches removed but which are painstakingly kept in place and which are described rather gloriously as 'veteran trees'.

Woodland Management

Planting and Protection

On the whole, we tend to take the permanent nature of trees for granted and then take notice only of situations where change has occurred. Of these, it is when the trees are at their smallest and least significant that they seem to make the most obvious impact on the local scenery, namely after they have been planted. In particular, it is the new trees put alongside roadways that stand out due to the plastic guards in which they are placed, looking rather like rows of multicoloured tombstones.

In most cases, new plantings are made with small saplings or 'transplants' that are raised in a nursery and then transplanted into the site during the winter months at a time when they are dormant and when there is least

Young trees protected by plastic guards

likelihood of their being damaged by drought. Once in the ground, however, the young trees are vulnerable to being eaten and to being smothered. The main threat of the former comes from rabbits, deer and farm animals and protection against them can be provided either by plastic guards as mentioned above or by fencing in the area or 'compartment' in which the planting has been done. Fencing against deer is the most noticeable as they can jump over heights of 2 metres or more, depending on whether they are the big red deer of Scotland or the smaller lowland varieties such as fallow or roe deer. Rabbit fences are much lower, but of a smaller mesh and will have been buried below the ground as well as stapled to posts above, since rabbits are of course good at burrowing! Farm animals, especially sheep, will be kept out by a run of wire netting with a strand of razor wire along the top.

The plastic tree guards provide individual protection and come in various designs according to what is required. As with fencing, guards against deer will be higher than those for rabbits and each is supported by a narrow wooden stake. These guards are now made from biodegradable materials that will also split to allow the stem of sapling to expand and grow. Guards tend to be used in small areas such as motorway verges that may be less easy to fence and also for plantations of broadleaf trees that respond better to the further protection that they give against weed and to the micro climate that can be created within them.

Fences and guards cannot, however, provide protection against one other potential source of damage, namely grey squirrels. These are of course great climbers and can be seen running up and down the trunks of trees and also flying, Tarzan-like, from branch to branch. Their main diet is nuts and seeds, which the forest can spare in plenty, but they also have a taste for stripping young bark, mainly from certain broadleaved trees. The bark, together with the layer of cambium that lies just beneath it, is an essential artery for a tree, connecting the two extreme parts of its nutritional process, the leaves and the roots. If this link is interrupted by a ring of bark being stripped away, then the tree will die. Squirrels are not only inclined to eat bark in this way, but will often do so at some height above the ground so that sizeable trees can be severely damaged and even killed. It is therefore particularly galling to lose trees in this way, as they may well by then be 20 years old or so and have been carefully tended for all that time. Rabbit damage is bad enough, but at least rabbits can only harm younger trees that are relatively easily replaced. Squirrels are difficult to control and can either be shot or caught in special hoppers that are designed so as not to trap other wildlife. Beech and sycamore are particularly vulnerable to attack by squirrels and several other species can be affected too.

Deer do their worst damage on the tender shoots of young trees as well, although they can also strip off bark from bigger trees either with their teeth or their antlers. The latter case arises when the stags try to remove the velvet off their antlers during the rutting season. This does not often encircle a tree and kill it, but it can cause a disfigurement that will reduce the value of the timber once it has matured.

Weeds have otherwise to be kept under control during the first few years, either by mechanical means using a brush cutter or strimmer or by spraying with a herbicide. As the trees are still small and planted close together (in rows about 2 metres apart) this has to be done by hand, using a knapsack sprayer. This and later management tasks require that trees are planted in rows, even though that can make the plantations look rather unnatural. Planted in this manner, the young trees grow close together to provide the best supportive growing environment, although as they mature they will become cramped and will need to be thinned.

Thinning and Felling

The other rather noticeable forestry operation is when chain saws are at work – even the very sound of the saws is somehow menacing and the sight of felled trees and the surrounding debris can appear rather destructive. In fact, this is almost always part of some essential work. If the trees are being felled, it is in order to make way for the next generation to be planted,

6 WOODS AND FORESTS

while if they are being thinned at an intermediary stage it is to allow the final crop of trees to grow to proper maturity. As mentioned just previously, the transplants have to be set close together if they are to thrive and, in a perfectly managed wood, 90% of these may be removed during their full life cycle so as to leave a final group of fully matured trees. To achieve this, the forester will need to take out an appropriate percentage of the growing trees every few years. This can either be done by felling complete rows of trees within the plantation or by selecting the individual stems that are either to remain or be removed, according to their position and condition. Such trees are often marked with a splash of paint or a number, which is not therefore a sign of vandalism but of a skilled managerial judgement made by the forester!

Such operations cost money and although the thinnings can be sold they may do little more than just cover those costs, particularly in the earlier stages when the size of the timber being taken out is small. The work might therefore only be justified if the final crop is likely to attract a quality market and command a premium price. It is not unusual therefore to see plantations where no regular thinning has taken place, especially in the more basic upland blocks of sitka spruce, with the result that the wood has become dark and enclosed and quite lifeless. By that stage, the area will have little or no wildlife and the timber will only be usable for the most basic purpose of pulp. The different types of timber and their uses is described briefly later in this chapter.

Forest harvester

In smaller woods and in the lowlands, felling and thinning are undertaken mostly with chain saws, but in the larger upland forests such work is now undertaken increasingly by specialist harvesting machines. These remarkable tractor units are fitted with hydraulic grabs incorporating a chain saw that can fell a tree and then hold it and turn it so that the side branches are trimmed off before then laying it in a stack or on a trailer. Being articulated, the unit can at the same time manoeuvre amongst the standing trees without causing damage. A far cry from the axes and cross-saws of only 50 years or so ago!

115

6 WOODS AND FORESTS

Rides and Firebreaks

Although woods can become densely overgrown, there are nonetheless situations where one may see wide openings running through the midst of the forest. These will be either grassy rides or made-up tracks, the latter providing access routes for machinery or fire-fighting equipment, but both allowing light into part of the wood and so creating conditions for a greater bio-diversity. In lowland or broadleaved woods, such rides may also be provided for shooting purposes, making effectively a clearing that pheasant will fly over and an area for the guns to stand.

Fire can spread throughout a whole forest unless it can be checked and one means of doing this is to leave a wide swathe of unplanted land. As the fire reaches the edge of the trees it is starved of further fuel and will die down and be more easily controlled. Forest fires are a particular hazard in the drier parts of the country and also in areas where there are more frequent visitors, as picnic fires, cigarette ends and broken glass are all potential dangers. Once it has taken hold and is probably also being fanned by the wind, the fire will be difficult to extinguish, due to the scale of the site, its remoteness and the probable lack of water. Some precautionary measures can be seen not only in the existence of hard tracks for use by fire engines but also in the form of occasional open water tanks or a collection of hand beaters, looking like long-handled shovels with rubber heads. Whilst these may seem rather diminutive measures, they can be effective once the fire has reached a clearing and is therefore reduced to a manageable level.

Pests and Diseases

A variety of pests and diseases can affect trees, but they are rarely as critical as when they occur in agricultural crops and it is unusual to see any action being taken against them, other than possible spraying with weedkiller. In fact, the causes and symptoms of these infestations in woods are more likely to be seen rather than signs of their eradication. The main source of attack is from fungi and insects. Toadstools are a common sight in the woods and most of them are harmless to growing trees. Some, however, do

6 WOODS AND FORESTS

work their way into the roots or into the cambium under the bark and start to clog the cells that constitute the living part of the timber. Many of these are hardly visible on the surface, being under the bark or below the ground, while others are easily noticed, such as the yellow pancake shapes of the honey fungus. The insects range from weevils and beetles that damage bark to caterpillars that eat into the leaves. Frequently these will all have emanated from dead wood and then spread into the living trees and one can often see where they will originally have been harboured.

Traditionally, when trees were thinned or felled, the ground would have been cleared of all the extraneous material such as the smaller branches, known as the lop and top, and even the stumps and roots. Nowadays, this tends all to be left on the site to rot, partly because to remove it is an extra expense on what is already a very marginal financial operation and partly because it provides a habitat for wildlife. Much of that wildlife is in fact just those beetles or fungi that then attack the trees that are still standing on the same site or have been newly planted there. Happily, such infestations are rarely fatal and are more likely only to reduce the quality and ultimate value of the timber. On balance, therefore, there is no need to clean up the forest floor and so remove the source of infestations. However, where certain species are particularly vulnerable, an insecticide may be applied to the old stumps which will then show as a green or similar stain. More often, foresters will have identified what the most likely risks would be in a particular plantation and will have selected a species that is resistant to them.

Whilst the control and eradication of disease may not have the same intensity in forestry as in agriculture, there are nonetheless cases when trees suffer some setback that causes them ultimately to die. The most pernicious of these is Dutch Elm Disease which devastated much of the English landscape in the late 1960s and is still endemic, as mentioned later. There are occasions too when oaks start to die back, becoming what is known as 'stag headed' due to the appearance of bare, dead branches at the tops of the trees. Latterly also, alders on river banks have begun to die. The cause

117

of such attacks is complex and often not conclusively identified. It is sometimes attributed to factors such as changes in climate or in the level and quality of water, and previously to the phenomenon of acid rain, but in certain cases it can also be traced to an increased vulnerability to specific diseases. The effects of such damage is generally more noticeable on trees growing in parks or hedgerows than within woods or forests, although the effects of fungal infestation might well be seen within conifer plantations where trees have lost their needles or become discoloured.

Sustainability

The policy within Britain which requires that trees may only be felled if the ground is replanted ensures that our timber is a constantly renewable resource. There has, however, been growing concern over such issues as the destruction of the rain forests in South America and the Far East from where much of our timber is imported. This has led to the establishment of an international code to determine that timber being sold around the world has been produced in a sustainable manner. Where this is being applied, the timber or the product made from it will be given a form of certification. Within Britain, and throughout much of Europe, this has now also been adopted in a manner that reflects the local circumstances. Woods and the system by which they are managed are inspected and then certified as meeting the accepted standards. This timber when felled and sold to processors and ultimately to retailers will therefore carry a certification as to the sustainable methods under which it was produced, as can now be seen on items being marketed in DIY and furniture stores.

There is another aspect of sustainability which is beginning to influence policy on tree planting, in that trees can absorb carbon dioxide and hold it effectively throughout their existence, even as milled timber, and ultimately until the wood is burnt. This is encouraging the planting of land beside busy roads or on the edge of urban areas with a view to improving air quality in those locations where there are heavy emissions of carbon dioxide.

6 WOODS AND FORESTS

Forest Trees

It is not the purpose of this book to provide an identification manual of British trees, as this can be readily found in other publications. It is, however, appropriate to refer to the main types of trees that are grown in this country and the uses to which they are put.

Travelling through central and southern England one will see mainly broadleaved trees interspersed with plantations of conifers. Within the woods, as opposed to the hedgerows, these will be predominantly oak,

beech or ash depending on the soils and conditions of each particular location. For example, in the Chilterns in Buckinghamshire the chalky ground favours beech, for which the area has been renowned for centuries. Further south and east into Surrey and Hampshire, the soils comprise clay which is better suited to oak. In forestry, the choice of what species to plant is made largely on what will grow well on that site and partly also on which type of timber will be most saleable once it matures. The same principles apply also to conifer plantations, although the outcome is rather less distinctive in the south of the country than in the uplands. Whilst there is a

6 WOODS AND FORESTS

wide diversity of conifers in the lowlands, including particularly varieties of larch and pine, many of these cannot thrive on higher ground so that commercial plantings in the hills have tended to rely extensively on one hardy species, namely sitka spruce. These basic commercial rules are now being tempered with a more environmental approach, so that efforts are being made to include a greater quantity of broadleaves in lowland plantings, where conifers may have been grown before, and to re-introduce native species to the highlands, such as the Caledonian pine and sessile oak. Meanwhile, the established woodland landscape does tend to reflect the planting policies of previous years with the frequent use of faster growing conifers. There is a limit, however, to where even the most hardy species can grow and hillsides that are particularly rocky or that rise over 400 or 500 metres above sea level tend to be bare of trees.

Some woods also demonstrate the commercial decisions that were made at the time of planting and which may not have produced the anticipated results at the stage when the crop matured. One can see sometimes examples of the attractive red oak that would have been planted perhaps 30 years ago in anticipation of a new source of hardwood but which has failed meanwhile to live up to expectations. Similarly, the tsuga or western hemlock was identified at one time as a conifer that would grow well throughout much of the country and was therefore chosen for planting in preference to, for example, the slower growing Douglas fir, but it now produces only an inferior timber that is difficult to sell.

Although plantations are usually made up of a specific mix of, say, two or three types of trees, there are other species that are often seen in established woods, either because they have sown themselves and been allowed to grow on or because the area has not been commercially managed. Sycamore, in particular, grows freely amongst other broadleaves, as does Spanish chestnut and wild cherry, and silver birch which will invade most woods if given the chance. Some varieties such as chestnut may well have originated from coppice, as described below.

6 WOODS AND FORESTS

Coppice

Coppicing is an ancient form of woodland practice that can still be seen and is indeed undergoing a degree of revival. A coppiced tree appears more like a bush than a tree in that it comprises wood that has been trained to grow out in a spread of stems that are then cut down at a relatively young stage and allowed to regrow. The original purpose of coppicing derives from the fact that timber production is such a slow process and that there was always a more immediate need for smaller cuts of wood, whether for fuel or for the making of articles such as fences, hurdles and wheel spokes. Certain types of tree, notably hazel and sweet chestnut, not only grow rapidly enough in their coppiced form to produce this smaller timber, but also respond to being cut by producing further growth. Furthermore, this can be done underneath established broadleaved trees such as oak, so that the woods then produce effectively a double crop.

Traditional oak wood with hazel coppice

Whilst there is far less demand now for coppice materials, the pattern of hazel or chestnut 'stools' can often still be seen within an oak wood, even if generally rather overgrown. Its preservation and continued management is being encouraged by the availability of grant aid and by a revival also of charcoal burning that makes good use of coppice. Charcoal is being made again by traditional methods in the broadleaved woods of southern England using kilns set up for the purpose on site. The burners are, however, still few in number and tend to be located in the midst of the woods and so are not readily encountered by the casual visitor!

Another means of gleaning smaller cuts of timber from forest trees was by pollarding. Whilst no longer practised for this purpose, its effects can still sometimes be seen in, for example, old oaks that have over the years formed a spread of branches low down rather than grown into a single tall stem. Such trees would have had their lower branches cut from time to time and then been allowed to regrow, providing a similar supply of wood to coppice but taking longer to do so and therefore being less commonly practised. Willows and other riverside trees are still pollarded but essentially now only to control their size and shape rather than to provide a supply of small timber. A similar process is used on roadside trees in towns.

Timber Products

Commercial

Remarkably for a product that is heavy and therefore costly to transport, almost 90% of the timber used in this country is imported from overseas. This is largely a matter of price, especially at a time when sterling is relatively strong. There are also advantages of scale in forest areas such as North America and Scandinavia and faster growing conditions in, for example, the tropics. As a result, the woodland resource within Britain is probably being under-utilised, although timber is nonetheless still being produced largely for commercial purposes. The end product for which it is used depends on the type of tree, the size and quality of the timber and on the prevailing market conditions.

At very best, an exceptional hardwood may be used for veneer, whereby a particularly fine oak or sycamore, for example, is put through a process that effectively peels the trunk into thin layers that are then used as high-quality facing for furniture. More usually, however, the hardwoods will be used either for joinery, if they are of a suitable type and quality such as a good beech, or for construction timber. The lesser grades and smaller sizes might be converted into fencing material or firewood. The better British softwoods tend to be aimed at the construction market and are rarely suitable for use in joinery. The lesser size and grade of softwoods are processed into panel products such as chipboard or used for pallets, pit props, fencing and rustic poles. Much of it is also used for pulping into paper and cardboard. Within these two broad categories of timber, there are specialisations, such as beech for furniture or Scots pine for telegraph poles.

When being converted into many of these products, the timber has first to be stripped of its bark, which was traditionally discarded as waste. It is now more often reduced into chips, together with much of the 'lop and top', and used for horticultural mulch or as a surface material for horse riding and pathways and sometimes also for making into panel boards.

Transport

Felled timber is transported generally by road and is of course readily noticeable by its size and by the fact that it is carried on uncovered trailers. Hardwoods tend to be in full-length trunks still with their distinctive bark, whereas the softwoods are often cut into uniform bars of 1.8 metres. These loads have to be taken to the saw mills and pulp mills which are located in the more wooded areas of the country, or even to a sea port, as much of Britain's pulp is in fact processed in Scandinavia.

Firewood

The upper branches of hardwoods are often cut into logs to be sold as firewood, as are whole trees that have been damaged or are in some way unfit for milling. Softwoods produce less unconvertible timber of this kind and are generally less well suited for use as firewood.

Farm Woods

It has already been mentioned how small blocks of woodland have evolved around the countryside and this is being perpetuated by new initiatives to plant trees on farms. The existing parcels of woodland have little commercial use compared to the larger areas described just previously and the purpose of the new plantings is largely to create an amenity or shooting cover. They are often noticeable due to the fact that, being largely broadleaves, they will have been placed inside plastic guards. Such plantings may be filling a corner of a field or extending a hedgerow or existing shelter belt. Much of this will have been instigated through grant aid under the Farm Woodland Premium Scheme or be part of a wider project such as one of the National Forests or Community Woods.

National Forests and Community Woods

There are areas of the country where road signs proclaim that one is entering a national or regional forest, but where the landscape then seems no more wooded than elsewhere. These are in fact projects, notably in central and southwestern England, for creating or extending woods within the existing countryside, so as to remake a traditional landscape where fields are interspersed with woods. The scheme is being used also to improve areas within the locality that have been scarred by past industrial use such as mining. These government-funded projects are relatively new and the trees will therefore still appear as young plantations.

Community woods are on a smaller scale and are being established also with government funding to create amenity areas of woodland within reach of towns or villages. Some of these were planted a few years ago so that the trees are now beginning to look quite sizeable and well established.

Park Trees

Not all trees are within woods or forests and many were planted as individual specimens in parkland on the old estates or left to grow there to provide shade for grazing livestock. Elsewhere, single trees can sometimes be seen standing in a rather forlorn line across an arable field. These could originally have been part of a hedge that had previously divided the field and which was then grubbed out, but where the trees were left standing either as a feature or, more probably, due to a preservation order. Whilst such trees may provide a memorial to a former landscape, they are often no longer a particularly attractive feature in themselves and can be of some hindrance to the farming of the land around them. Not only do individual trees, like electricity pylons, interrupt the line of arable work, but the trees also cause shade and take up moisture and nutrients from the soil which would otherwise be used by the crops. The more current policy of planting up small areas of woods on farms, as described above, is likely to provide a more balanced landscape than retaining single trees.

Older trees that have been left standing in this way or which form part of a small wood or copse may often be covered in ivy. This gives an impression of neglect and even decay. Whether ivy does in fact damage trees is never quite clear, but the general view is that there is no need to clear the ivy other than on visual grounds and that often the reason it has taken hold is because the tree was already weakened or dying.

7 HEDGEROWS, PATHS AND BRIDLEWAYS

Hedgerows

There has been much comment over the years about the many miles of hedgerows that have been removed from the English landscape. Some of these statements may have been enhanced by a rather forceful use of statistics, but it is nonetheless clear that the development of larger machinery and new farming techniques during the mid- and late twentieth century created a need for larger fields, especially in the arable areas. At one time, this kind of rationalisation was even considered important enough to warrant being financially encouraged through government grants. The drive towards maximising output and efficiency meant that it was no longer practical to work within small fields where modern equipment was unable to manoeuvre successfully. Furthermore, the farms best suited to arable cultivation were tending to concentrate on crop production and were giving up their livestock and ploughing in the grassland. The old hedges had served as a stock-proof boundary between fields, but once they were no longer needed for that purpose they would appear just to be taking up ground that could now be growing crops instead. Not only did hedges take up space, but they would also harbour weeds and wildlife such as rabbits that would spread into the fields. In areas such as parts of Suffolk one can see where this was taken to extremes, with the removal even of boundary hedges and the crops then being grown right up to the roadside verges. In many cases where hedges have been grubbed out, the countryside still appears somehow denuded and spoiled. Elsewhere it may no longer be quite so noticeable, although it will have resulted in a permanent loss of habitat for wildlife.

It might be assumed that hedges have always formed an intrinsic part of the British countryside and indeed the field patterns in England do show a marked contrast to the rest of Europe, as can be seen so clearly when flying into the country from the Continent. In fact much of this landscape dates from the mid-eighteenth and nineteenth centuries, resulting from the Parliamentary Enclosure Acts of the time. There are also some areas where the landscape has been without hedgerows for many centuries and where the open country has its own particular beauty, especially when viewed in terms of the farming that is being carried out there. This applies to, for example, the fens of eastern England and the carrs of the north west. Here, where the land is level and low lying, the fields are divided by ditches and dykes rather than hedges or fences. They comprise some of the best arable soils in the country and are cultivated usually to very high standards, often with specialised crops such as celery, radishes or beetroot that cannot be grown successfully elsewhere. Although not benefiting from the traditional patchwork of hedges, these highly commercial areas have a rare beauty of their own, as well as their own wildlife, such as water birds.

Elsewhere, the trend for removing hedges appears to have been reversed, especially on roadsides where lines of new thorn plants sheathed within plastic rabbit guards can often be seen. Indeed, under the Hedgerow Regulations 1997, no one may remove a hedge without first notifying the local authority who then have powers to insist on it being retained, provided that it is of sufficient historic or local importance. Part of the value of farm hedges is the diversity of species that can grow within them and the habitat that they provide for wildlife. Most of these, such as hawthorn, hazel or ash, are deciduous plants that can, when properly maintained, provide a thick stock-proof border throughout the year, in marked contrast to so many garden hedges that rely on unnatural-looking evergreens like Lawson Cypress. Farm hedges need to be cut each year if they are to retain their proper shape and purpose and if they are not to spread out too far or become tall and open. Often this is now done with a tractor-mounted flail which produces initially a rather ragged result that does, however, grow over into a neat finish during the following spring. The more traditional practice of 'laying' hedges is being revived, although it is far more demanding in both time and skill than using a mechanised flail. The way in which this is done varies from region to region, but basically it involves splitting the stems of the bushes, bending them down and weaving them along the horizontal, so that they form a living latticed fence. When

7 HEDGEROWS, PATHS AND BRIDLEWAYS

The trend in modern arable farming, as discussed in Chapter 2, is to make the most economical use of machinery in order to produce crops that are of a consistently high quality. At the same time, there is an increasing tendency to leave the headlands uncultivated or in setaside. A path that runs through the middle of a field causes an interference to this style of arable work and fails to use the uncultivated areas that may have been left around the edge.

A pathway that is left undisturbed will cause weeds to spread into the crop and yet if it is ploughed with the rest of the field and kept free of weed it is more likely to become muddy when walked over. Often a path that cuts across an arable field will have to be sprayed with herbicide in order to keep it clear, which may be practical but not necessarily everyone's ideal for walking in the country. Straying off a path, whether by people or their dogs, will of course cause damage to the crop, especially towards harvest time. On grassland farms, too, there can be damage to growing forage crops such as hay and silage, although the concern is more with livestock being disturbed or being let out if gates are left open. Dogs that chase farm animals may only rarely actually attack them, but even the playful chase

7 HEDGEROWS, PATHS AND BRIDLEWAYS

can have fatal consequences to pregnant ewes. Within woods, the possibility of game birds being scattered and even killed is considered further in Chapter 8.

There are many stories about extreme behaviour in regard to footpaths or bridleways; whether of farmers blocking off a legitimate route or of ramblers trampling down a growing crop. There are also cases where seemingly unreasonable legal rights are enforced, when, for example, evidence of vehicular use in the distant past, meaning a horse and cart, is the basis for opening up an old green lane to joy-riding by four-wheel drive cars. Even the official names given to some rights of ways sound unreal, such as BOATs (Byways Open to All Traffic) and RUPPs (Roads Used as Public Paths). In general, where public rights exist, most farmers have been ready to accommodate those who wish to use them. Some have even created new ones, in the form of pay-as-you-go bridleways or as part of Countryside Stewardship Schemes. In many cases, too, farmers and landowners have co-operated with local schemes in having waymarks and signboards erected along the route of paths.

Strangely, since fences and gates are crucial for keeping stock safely within whatever area they are supposed to be grazing or sheltering, the tradition among British farmers has often been to use rather makeshift arrangements with wire and twine rather than erect proper gates or stiles. These may appear rather unwelcoming to any visitor who has to struggle with frayed knots and loops of barbed wire, or to heave at an old gate that has sunk on its hinges. It also raises the likelihood of the 'gate' not being shut properly or of fencing wire being pressed down as people are forced to climb over it – and then leaving a similar opportunity for the livestock too!

However, as farming conditions have become increasingly difficult, bringing a greater need for efficiency and a reduction in the numbers working in agriculture, so too does it become harder to absorb some of the potential losses or additional management tasks that are involved in maintaining

public paths across private land. At the same time, there are more people visiting the countryside and hence there is a growing need for recreational facilities such as paths and bridleways. New legislation is to give greater freedom to roam across open areas, such as mountains and moors, but this does not aim to deal with enclosed farmland or with woods and forests. In these excepted cases, allowing best use to be made of the existing paths and at the same time enabling the land over which they pass to be properly managed will still depend on a high degree of mutual understanding.

8 FIELD SPORTS

Shooting

Shooting tends to take place at some distance from roads and paths, partly for reasons of safety and largely because it is in the deeper country that there will be the necessary habitat or 'cover' for the birds and the right terrain for the shooters. It is therefore only occasionally that any direct evidence of the sport may be seen in the landscape, other than in some of the more permanent features such as the shelter belts, butts and areas of game crops mentioned previously. As with all field sports, shooting takes place within a set season so that the guns would only be seen (or heard) during that time, even though the gamekeeper's tasks run throughout the year.

Keepering

The gamekeeper has ultimately to ensure that a sufficient number of birds are available throughout the season and in the right places. Where these are 'wild birds' or those naturally raised on the property, as with all grouse and most duck and partridge, this will be a case of controlling predators, maintaining the habitat and also providing feed and medication when necessary. One vivid example of maintaining habitat is in the burning of heather as mentioned in Chapter 5 while others such as managing woodland undergrowth are less noticeable. Another rather traditional sign that might still be encountered occasionally in the woods is that of a gamekeepers' 'larder' where the vermin and predators that have been caught or shot are strung up as evidence of his diligence or as a sinister warning to other crows or weasels! One less visible sign that keepering has taken place may well be in the improvement of some species of wildlife, such as songbirds, that might otherwise suffer from inadequate habitats or from exposure to predators.

Rearing Pheasant

In most pheasant shoots the majority of birds will have been reared or 'put down' either as chicks or as young birds or 'poults'. Evidence of this may be encountered within a wood where a rearing area has been carefully fenced in, so as to provide protection against foxes and other predators and

provided with a second gun, ready loaded with cartridges, so as to enable a more rapid rate of fire. With them, too, may be a 'picker up' with one or two dogs which are trained to seek out any birds that have fallen either at some distance away or into undergrowth and to bring them to the shooter. The guns are given precise positions at which to stand that will have been marked out by a stick with a number attached to it. These markers can often be seen out in the fields or around a wood and are an indication that the land is being used for a shoot.

The fact that the guns are given such precise positions is mainly to ensure that they are in line with where the birds are expected to fly and are spaced out so that each has a safe and adequate field of fire. In such cases, the pheasant are 'driven' from their cover towards the guns by a team of 'beaters' (who beat the trees and undergrowth in order to create a disturbance, rather than beating the birds themselves!). Each 'drive' will have been designed as far as possible so that the birds will rise up in flight as they

8 FIELD SPORTS

break cover rather than run along the open ground. The convention of shooting is that only birds in flight may be shot. This can be achieved by natural means such as clearing an inner area of undergrowth or leaving a belt of trees or by introducing some material like torn-up plastic fertiliser bags which are then strung up like bunting or small flags. These might also be festooned discreetly within the edge of a wood to discourage the birds from straying away from where they are being 'held' in preparation of a drive.

Another design feature of a shoot is that when one drive has been completed, those birds that have escaped the guns should have somewhere behind in which to land, like a wood or shelter belt. The beaters can then be brought round to the far side of that cover and drive the birds back again in the opposite direction.

The beaters on a pheasant shoot may be largely out of sight in woods or undergrowth, but they can often be heard as they shout, whistle and bang sticks in order to flush the birds out before them. They will, however, be seen on the move between drives, usually on a trailer drawn behind a tractor and covered with a makeshift roof or cabin. The shooting season takes place between October and February and some protection from the wintry weather is going to be welcome!

A partridge shoot that takes place in more open ground can also involve the use of beaters, with the birds being flushed out of low cover like scrub or game crops and driven over ditches or hedges towards the guns. In this more open country it is also more feasible for the guns to walk out over the land and shoot such birds as may rise before them. Pheasants, too, can be shot without the use of beaters, in what is termed rough shooting.

Grouse

The same applies to grouse shooting, although this takes place in the very different terrain of moorland. The grouse is unique to Britain and survives only on the moors of Scotland and north England and in some parts of

Wales. It depends entirely upon breeding naturally in the wild, but is then aided as much as possible by good keepering in controlling predators, improving habitat and providing feed and even medication. Living in a relatively harsh environment, grouse are vulnerable to suffering losses due to disease and even drowning when the chicks are overwhelmed by spring rains. In some years the numbers may be so reduced that shooting will even be abandoned for that season. In better times, however, the shoot follows a similar practice to that of partridge, in that the birds may either be driven or 'walked'. Driven grouse is the most favoured and the guns will be seen in the 'butts', often with their loaders and someone to pick up. The beaters meanwhile walk out in line over the moor to flush the birds out of the heather to fly over the butts.

Deer Stalking

Scotland is renowned also for deer stalking, which is not, however, a particularly visible activity. The red deer breed naturally in parts of the Highlands in what are referred to as deer forests but are now almost entirely bare hillsides. Stalking is a method of controlling the development of a herd by culling specific animals, primarily the stags but also some of the older or weaker hinds. It is done on foot, although backed up with an all-terrain vehicle or a pony, and involves just the shooter and the 'stalker' who is the equivalent of a keeper and will have monitored the state of the herd and the movement of the stags. This tends to be in extremely remote places and has to be done in a quiet and skilful manner with the deer being literally stalked as if by a wild hunting animal. It is therefore rarely seen by most visitors to the Highland countryside.

Other types of deer are becoming increasingly numerous in lowland areas too and are also 'stalked' although in a more contained manner. Roe deer, as well as fallow and muntjac, are now common in woods throughout much of England and have even become a pest to foresters, farmers and gardeners. Evidence of the shooting of such deer takes the form of a rudimentary perch or 'high seat' which may have been erected in a

8 FIELD SPORTS

Fallow deer

woodland clearing. It is likely to comprise a basic ladder with a small platform upon which the shooter can sit out of sight and smell of any deer that may pass through the clearing below. Although the range is much closer than when stalking red deer on the hill, the roe deer stalker must still use a rifle in order to ensure a clean kill. A rifle bullet travels a huge distance if it misses its target and would be dangerous to use in a wood, where a shooter cannot see over the same wide distances as in the open hills, and in a more populous area, where it could strike someone in the locality. Shooting from above, out of a high seat, ensures not only that one can see the quarry without it being alerted but also that if the shot misses, the bullet will go harmlessly into the ground. Furthermore, woodland stalking tends to take place very early in the morning, when most dog walkers may still be safely in bed!

8 FIELD SPORTS

Ground Game

This is a rather traditional expression that refers to animals such as rabbit and hare that are not considered part of a formal shoot and which may be shot by the occupier of the land, generally the farm tenant, rather than the holder of the sporting rights. Foxes are also sometimes shot when known to be causing damage or when their numbers are not being adequately controlled by the hunt, but this would not be considered to be game shooting.

Guns

Game birds, wildfowl and pigeon are all shot with shotguns in which the cartridges are filled with numerous small metal pellets that scatter as soon as they are fired out of the barrel. This gives one a greater chance of striking a small and fast-moving target such as a bird in flight, whilst still being capable of killing it cleanly too. The shot does not, however, travel nearly as far or as fast as a rifle bullet and is soon spent and harmless. Nonetheless, shotguns are potentially lethal, especially when close to, and all sportsmen are required to observe a very strict safety code. Indeed, when they are moving between stands their guns will be 'broken', with the barrels hinged open and away from the trigger mechanism. Also, when the stands are within sight of a road, probably only the backs of the shooters will be seen as their line of fire will be arranged so as to be away from where the public might be.

A shotgun is not sufficient to kill a deer reliably, particularly when fired from a distance, and a rifle has therefore to be used for stalking.

The Shooting Seasons

Shooting is restricted to specific open seasons, mainly in order to protect the birds during mating and breeding. For pheasant, the season runs from October 1 to February 1, although most shoots wait until about November when the poults will have matured fully and when the more wintry weather should have made the birds more active. Towards the end of the season, the day's shooting may be restricted to 'cocks only' with a view to preserving an adequate number of breeding hens for the next year. Partridge begins at the beginning of September and finishes on the same day as the pheasant season. The grouse season opens promptly on the famous Glorious 12th of August and runs officially until December 10, although most shooting would have been completed before then. The number of times that shooting can take place during the season depends essentially on how many drives there are and how readily the birds can be prepared for further activity. On a large estate, this might be once each week or, on an ordinary farm shoot, perhaps just 8 or 10 times in the season.

Shooting would traditionally have been a pastime for the local landowners and farmers and their friends. It is now enjoyed by a far wider range of people, many of whom may be from a city or corporate background, and is often let out at substantial rents. In doing so, there is a presumption that the quality of sport will be commensurate with the level of rent being paid and with the expectations of those participating. This is especially so in the more accessible areas such as southern England and has created pressure to rear larger numbers of birds and also to have shoots on as many days as possible. It would explain, too, why there seem to be such large numbers of pheasants around prior to the season and the protective attitude towards them that is taken by those whose responsibility they are.

In contrast to the current trend with so many other sporting pastimes, there is a convention still that game shooting does not take place on Sundays.

Fishing

Coarse Fishing

The most visible image of fishing in England is of anglers seated at almost regular intervals on the banks of rivers, protected by large green umbrellas. The fact that they are fishing from a set position on the riverside rather than working their way along the bank or in the water, indicates that they are 'coarse' as opposed to 'game' fishing. This is determined by the nature of the river and what is likely to be living within it. Coarse fish encompass a diverse range of indigenous species such as roach, tench, perch and pike, most of which are no longer considered palatable by modern tastes, and the catch is therefore always returned to the water. One exception to this is pike, which does get cooked and eaten and which is, furthermore, a voracious eater of other fish and may therefore be removed from the river to help preserve stocks. Other indications, even when there are no fishermen present, are the small clearings made to give them the necessary access to the edge of the water and signs that might be posted up stating that the fishing rights are held by a local angling club. Coarse fishing also takes place on still water such as lakes or flooded mineral workings, which will have been stocked not only with the ordinary species of fish but also sometimes with carp that can grow to a very large size and therefore produce a special sporting challenge. The coarse fishing season runs from June 16 through to the following March 14.

Game Fishing

Game fishing is generally less noticeable in that it tends to be done in greater isolation and with the angler more on the move than coarse fishing. It is also confined to a more limited number of rivers and lakes as the fish survive only in certain types of water, much of which is in relatively remote areas of the country. One way of distinguishing game fishing is that the anglers are constantly casting their lines across the water from the bank, or as they wade in the water, or even from a boat.

Trout

Trout survive only in clean water with a low acidity such as is associated with chalk streams, although they also thrive in the peaty lochs and rivers of Wales and Scotland. There is little physical evidence of where trout may be fished for sport, other than perhaps from a notice stating 'private fishing' and the existence occasionally of shallow timber weirs that have been laid across the stream. This is to control the movement of the fish along the river which will have been divided nominally, if not actually physically, into sections or 'beats' within which individual anglers will be entitled to fish.

_8_ FIELD SPORTS

Another such feature may be in the form of groynes built out from the banks to improve the flow of water. A trout stream will in fact be managed in much the same way as a pheasant shoot, even to the extent of introducing reared fish to the water to increase the numbers. Management may involve cutting weed in the water, which can hide the fish, trimming trees and undergrowth around the banks which might otherwise impede an angler from casting his line, and keeping the river clear of pike. These tasks would traditionally be undertaken by a riverkeeper or ghillie.

Trout are also found in still water, whether in the wild as would be the case in, for example, the Scottish lochs or in specially stocked artificial lakes such as flooded gravel pits. Unlike coarse fish, trout can be fished from a boat as well as off the bank and therefore the presence of a boathouse or the sight of anglers drifting across the lake would be a sign that the water contains trout.

There is another species known as sea trout which, despite its name, is found in rivers or estuaries. It does, however, spend part of its life out at sea and is therefore fished in much the same way as salmon.

Salmon

Salmon are associated predominantly with Scotland but are also found in the larger rivers of Wales and in the south west of England. They are entirely wild and migrate up the rivers from the sea. There will again be little physical evidence of where salmon are being fished, especially as this will often be in relatively remote locations, although there may be a small shed or 'bothy' along the banks to provide shelter for the fishermen. They themselves might be seen standing perhaps waist deep in the full flow of the stream whilst casting into an otherwise inaccessible 'pool' where a particular fish is thought to be.

Game Fishing Seasons

Salmon and sea trout may be fished between February 2 and November 1 and the season for trout runs from March 2 until October 1.

difference between hunting a live quarry and pursuing a laid scent trail, drag hunting brings no benefit to the farmers over whose property it passes although still causing damage to the land and hedges.

Beagling

Another form of hunting that has always been done on foot and which may occasionally be seen in the open country is beagling. The quarry in this case is a hare and the beagles are controlled by huntsmen with horns, wearing traditional hunting livery, in a very similar way to fox hunting.

Hunt Kennels

Hounds and beagles are kept in hunt kennels, which may look like a rather unremarkable small farmyard, and in which they are then cared for and exercised throughout the year. The hounds are traditionally fed on meat taken off farm animals which have died and which are now increasingly difficult to dispose of, and the kennels are looked upon as providing an important service in this respect.

Coursing

Coursing involves fewer numbers of people and is far less common than other forms of hunting. Furthermore, it usually takes place in relatively remote areas such as open downland and so is rarely seen. In this case, the quarry is again the hare which is pursued by dogs that are famed for their speed rather than their scenting ability, such as lurchers and greyhounds, working individually or in pairs rather than in a pack as in the case of foxhounds and beagles. In its proper form, coursing follows a clear code of conduct and is a matter of judging a dog's ability to chase a hare that, when sighted, will always be given about a 70-metre lead. There is, however, also an illegal version of coursing, which is carried out by a different kind of enthusiast who does not observe such rules, and is usually carried out rather covertly at dawn or dusk.

9 BEHIND THE SCENERY

The People

The foregoing chapters have dealt largely with what is to be seen in the country, such as the crops and stock, but there should now also be some mention of the people in whose care all this lies. There is no stereotyped farmer and it would be quite presumptuous to make any generalised comments about the rural population, although it may be helpful to mention something about its past and how the land tends now to be owned or occupied.

Cattle auction

One hundred years ago, 90% of farms in Britain were owned by landlords and let to tenants. Now most are owner-occupied and only about 30% are let on long-term leases. The majority of farms are therefore run and financed as private, often family, businesses. Those that are tenanted are generally on annual leases that run for the lifetime of the tenant and even, under some circumstances, for that of the succeeding generation too. Indeed, up until 1995, the law in England and Wales still presumed that leases of agricultural land would have to be on that long-term basis and allowed only few opportunities for letting land on shorter terms. In Scotland, leases have also been generally for the lifetime of the tenant although other, more commercial, arrangements for fixed term occupation were available. Under current legislation, farm tenancies can be arranged for whatever period is agreed between the two parties and new lettings do now average around four years. These tend, however, to be used in cases where land is being taken by someone in addition to an existing farm as a means of improving the scale of their prevailing operations. The question of long-term security is then not as crucial as it would be in the case where the property is both the home and sole source of livelihood for the tenant. Traditionally, however, whether farmers own their property or are tenants under the old statutory system, there is a very close identity with the land and with the ongoing responsibility for its management. The tenanted land may either be in private hands, such as the old aristocratic families or more recently trust funds, or otherwise be owned by a corporate body or

147

9 BEHIND THE SCENERY

institution such as the Crown or Church or one of the Oxbridge colleges, or a public body such as a County Council or the Ministry of Defence. Virtually all land is in some such ownership, whether on a remote hillside or indeed 'common land' which, despite its name, is privately owned and subject to rights of occupation by specified local 'commoners'.

The rise in owner occupation during the last century came about largely due to the impact of Death Duties, when the old estates were often sold and split up, and also due to the high degree of security afforded to tenants. This security was intended as a means of providing stability to the vital business of food production, following the slump of the 1930s and the privations of the Second World War. However, it had the further effect that when farms were vacated by tenants, generally only upon their death, they would probably not be relet for another whole lifetime but taken in hand instead. During the most recent agricultural recession, there has been a tendency for farms to be amalgamated in order for one party to gain economies of scale and for the other to be able perhaps to retire. Taken overall, the farming population is an ageing one, as the family farm can no longer always support two generations with sons or daughters working alongside their parents, as would have happened previously. Also, the younger generation have other opportunities available to them that can offer financially more rewarding returns and often for less hard work and heartache. This is not to imply that British farming is necessarily showing signs of age or lack of resources. Throughout history, farmers have been remarkably resilient and resourceful, as well as traditional, and the challenges of the last years have been met with innovation and continuing modernisation. The calibre and commitment of Young Farmers Clubs around the country are one indication of this determination. There are, furthermore, large commercial enterprises operating alongside the smaller, more traditional farms. Some of the latter have rationalised and are using contractors for all or some of their work, so that big modern machinery can be seen at work in situations where such equipment could not otherwise have been afforded. This will also be the case where land has been amalgamated, as mentioned just previously.

9 BEHIND THE SCENERY

There has been a trend too in recent years for farmers to supplement their agricultural incomes by some outside means, whether through diversification, as discussed in Chapter 10, or by someone within the family taking employment elsewhere. Again, this remedy to an otherwise unprofitable situation will not really be noticeable to anyone from outside, as the farm will still be occupied and seemingly well managed. Some of these farms are effectively becoming part-time holdings, in a way that is already more commonplace in continental Europe where the unit size is generally smaller, and therefore less viable, than in Britain. Another tendency towards part-time farming arises with the growing influx of people buying country properties and occupying it in conjunction with another business interest.

Country cottages are a further indicator of the changing pattern of farming. Prior to mechanisation, agriculture relied upon an extensive manual labour force and, as most farms were in relatively remote locations, these workers tended to live on the farm. Transport too was less easy than it might be now for the modern-day workers who may well have their own car. Farms and estates would therefore have their own cottages in which to accommodate staff. Over the years, the numbers needed to work on the land declined and their cottages became vacant and were either sold or let to people unconnected with farming. Indeed, just recently with the decline in agricultural incomes and the corresponding rise in residential values, many estates are receiving more in cottage rents than from their farming returns.

At the other end of the scale are the large country houses and former stately homes. Previously these, and a whole army of estate workers, would have been sustained largely by the income derived from the surrounding land. Over the years, however, the rising costs of maintaining such properties and the decline in farming returns has meant that many such houses are now separated from the original estate and are in private or commercial occupation. The land will meanwhile probably have been incorporated into neighbouring farms, leaving just the original park around the house itself. Where the big houses have been converted to a corporate use, whether as offices or hotels or nursing homes, they once again attract a workforce. However, these workers tend to drive in from homes that may be some distance away and their presence is not therefore quite the same as the community of estate workers of old. Interestingly, at a time when there has been resistance against developing new homes in rural areas, planning policy has favoured the construction of new country houses in a style that might echo the old stately homes. There are a few instances, therefore, where sumptuous new houses have been built, sometimes on the site of one that was demolished years ago following the break-up of an estate. Whilst these may look the part of a former manor house, they are unlikely in the present day to be able to embrace the wider role of the traditional estate as the centre of a whole community.

Farmers and landowners are effectively the front line of the countryside behind whom there is a whole range of people whose livelihoods are also intimately bound up with it. Those who work the land itself are a diminishing number, due to the economies afforded by ever greater mechanisation and latterly also due to the effects of recession. Mention has been made previously of how it can be more efficient to contract out farm work rather than use one's own labour and machinery. These contractors therefore form an important feature of the 'second line' of farming people, as do the vets and agronomists or the machinery dealers and other merchants. Land agents and auctioneers, as well as accountants and solicitors, are also a part of what makes up the working countryside. Farming can appear to be lonely when one sees a single tractor ploughing a large and empty field, but the driver within it is a bit like the visible tip of an iceberg supported by a larger mass of people who are mostly hidden from view.

9 BEHIND THE SCENERY

Europe and the Common Agricultural Policy

The Common Agricultural Policy

In the context of this book it can only really be feasible to offer a brief observation on the workings of the Common Agricultural Policy and to comment on the way that it is perceived and how it may have influenced the rural landscape. To give a proper assessment of this remarkable institution would require at least another volume on its own!

One of the principles upon which the original European Economic Community was founded in the aftermath of the Second World War was that there should be a secure and stable supply of food, at a reasonable price to the consumers whilst also providing a reasonable income to the producers. At that time, the Community numbered only six members and these aims were achievable through a system of price support and intervention buying. As the Community grew not only in number but also in diversity, this became more difficult and created a situation in which vast surpluses of foodstuffs were having to be stored in what became known as 'mountains' and 'lakes' of, for example, butter and wine. The fact that farmers were effectively guaranteed a certain price on whatever they produced gave an understandable incentive to grow as much as they could. This encouraged increasingly intensive systems of production and also brought what would previously have been marginal land into cultivation. In retrospect, it can now be seen that this caused an environmental loss, whether through the ploughing up of old pastures or the greater use of chemicals and fertilisers. The pressure for change came from several directions, as the existing arrangements were not only extremely costly but also politically unsatisfactory both within Europe and in the context of World Trade Agreements. By 1992 a package of reforms was finally introduced whereby the level of financial support would be gradually reduced and no longer paid according to the amount produced but linked instead to the area upon which the crops were being grown. Payments were even offered on land that was to be left fallow or 'setaside', in an effort to reduce the surpluses.

Overall, these newer policies had to be welcomed as an improvement on what had gone before, although there were still many anomalies. Above all it seemed that, under setaside, farmers were being paid for doing nothing or, worse still, for letting their land become derelict. In actual fact, there are management requirements and environmental benefits with setaside, which are touched upon in Chapter 2. Other consequences of the new regime may have been noticed in the spread of oilseed rape across much of the country, as the different market arrangements for such crops meant that subsidies continued to encourage further production. The changing emphasis in agricultural policy has resulted also in the introduction of further funding for environmental measures, whose influence might well be seen in, for example, increased tree planting under the Farm Woodland Premium Scheme or the Countryside Stewardship Scheme. The continued existence of many hill farms in Britain is also now largely due to special funding that is made available in those areas, albeit coupled with a proviso of reducing the numbers of sheep and cattle being grazed. Meanwhile, the consequences for the agricultural industry as a whole could be that the pendulum is swinging too far. The policy of 'extensification' or reducing the numbers grazed on each hectare, as just mentioned, will have the effect of reducing income to livestock farmers. The remaining system of price support, through 'intervention' buying, is controlled by governments setting certain requirements and standards, and is subject to change and will not therefore be assured for all crops.

Within the UK, farmers happen to be labouring under additional burdens. Firstly, the European Commission payments are assessed in euros so that the level of payments received in Britain has effectively been discounted as the value of sterling has remained high. Secondly, much of the new grant aid from Europe is dependent upon the British Government matching those payments with an equivalent amount funded from national resources, which has not always been forthcoming. Thirdly, there is a culture within the UK of following rules to the letter, so that every aspect of policy has to be adhered to even when elsewhere in Europe they may be taking a

9 **B E H I N D   T H E   S C E N E R Y**

more pragmatic view. This applies particularly to some of the more difficult and frustrating regulations involving, for example, health and safety or exhaustive form filling. Fourthly, as part of the overall reform of the CAP there is the intention to restrict payments according to the size of a farm, under a principle known as 'modulation'. Farms in Britain tend to be larger than those throughout much of the rest of Europe, for reasons mentioned in Chapter 1, and it is likely therefore that many of these businesses will in future have their grant and subsidy payments capped.

European Regional Development Programme (ERDP)

A further part of the recent reforms is to introduce a whole package of funding for environmental schemes and for commercial purposes, such as processing, marketing and diversification. This last aspect is referred to in Chapter 10 and is likely to be the most visible consequence of the changing nature of rural policy, as barns are converted to non-farming uses or as land is planted with trees or used to grow energy crops, for example. The range of projects covered by the ERDP is summarised in the next section.

Grants and Subsidies

The overall impression that many will have of agriculture within the EU is that of farmers being 'featherbedded' and receiving all sorts of grants and subsidies. Some of this has been put into perspective by the observations of the preceding sections and whilst it is not possible here to quantify what such support means to each farming business, it may be useful just to itemise very briefly the main types of payments made.

Agricultural

Arable Aid Payments

Annual payments made on all land registered as arable, on a per hectare basis, introduced in lieu of direct price support and dependent on adopting setaside.

9 BEHIND THE SCENERY

Setaside
>   Annual payment for land left out of agricultural cultivations according
>   to prevailing requirements.

Beef and Sheep Premiums
>   Annual payments made per head of livestock, effectively to compensate
>   for low market prices. Dependent on certain conditions as to timing,
>   stocking rates and localities, including the raising of suckler herds.

Milk Quota
>   Cows' milk can only be sold into the public market provided the
>   producer has a quota for a particular annual amount. A levy imposed
>   if quota exceeded. There is no price support on dairy output.

Hill Livestock Compensatory Amounts
>   Being replaced by Hill Farm Allowance.

Agri-environmental

Environmentally Sensitive Areas
>   Where farmers opt for low-input systems they can receive payment
>   in compensation for nominal loss of production.

Countryside Stewardship Scheme
>   Grants available towards costs associated with works to improve
>   conservation and access.

Organic Farming Scheme
>   Aid towards costs associated with period of conversion to
>   organic farming.

Woodland Grant Scheme
>   Payment of grants towards cost of restocking felled woodlands and for
>   various woodland conservation schemes.

Farm Woodland Premium Scheme
>   Payment of grants for new tree planting.

Hill Farm Allowance
>   Annual subsidy to help sustain viability of upland management, linked
>   to stocking rates and to environmental requirements and now assessed
>   on a per hectare basis.

Sites of Special Scientific Interest (SSSIs)
> Where constraints are imposed on an area of land to protect rare or valuable fauna and flora, grants may be payable to compensate for loss of agricultural or forestry income.

Project-based

Processing & Marketing
> Start-up grant towards costs of developing processing units.

Rural Enterprise
> Grant support for setting up new ventures in rural regions.

Energy Crops
> Grant aid for the establishment of power stations and fuel crops.

Vocational Training
> Funding for training in non-farming businesses.

Others

Locational Supplements
> Some additional rates of grant are payable in specified areas, such as Less Favoured Areas for livestock, Special Conservation Areas or Challenge Areas for woods.

Unsupported Crops
> There is no agricultural grant support for root crops or fruit and vegetables, nor for pigs or poultry.

Enlargement

There is a commitment within the existing EU to extend the membership to include a number of central and eastern European states at such time as economic and other conditions will allow. The first tranche of this expansion may occur in 2003 or 2004 and would introduce a new dimension to the CAP, especially as some of the potential new member countries such as Hungary and Poland have a significant agricultural output. This could probably only be absorbed through further rationalisation of the present system, involving further reductions in support payments to farmers throughout the EU.

Conservation

In addition to the environmental schemes such as the tree planting grants mentioned earlier, there are a number of conservation measures being implemented by the European Commission under the terms of various international agreements. These concern primarily the protection of habitats for migratory birds and require each country to designate special areas where such habitats will be preserved. Such sites tend to be on coastal marshes and similar areas that are not particularly suited for intensive agricultural cultivation, although they can also be on open arable or downland. Some of them would already have been designated within the UK as being Sites of Special Scientific Interest so that there is now a danger that additional areas will need to be identified merely in order to fulfil the agreed international quota.

Farming in the Foodstores

There are occasionally stories reported in the media about how school-children seem to know so little about the way in which food is produced and that when asked, for example, where milk comes from, they reply that it is out of bottles or cartons. The reaction to such articles is usually that children should be better educated and encouraged to expand their horizons. Certainly it seems absurd not to know even the most basic facts about food production, but it is perhaps difficult sometimes to make the link between the cellophaned packages on the supermarket shelves and the crops and animals being raised in the countryside outside.

There are a number of reasons for this apparent difficulty: the fact that most of the agricultural produce that we consume is in a processed form; the pristine way in which other items such as meat, fruit and vegetables are presented for sale; the fact that the range of foods being offered is roughly the same throughout the year, whereas farming changes so much with the seasons; and that there are so many imported products even though there seems to be such an ample supply in our own country.

Processed food, even in a staple form such as bread, bears no resemblance to the wheat that it has been made from and it is understandable then not to make the connection between, for example, a pint of beer and a crop of malting barley. But even fruit and vegetables, in their raw and uncooked state, are presented in such a clean and uniform manner that it is difficult to remember that they were originally grown on muddy and windswept fields! Gone even is the practice of dusting potatoes with a black soil to make it look as if they had been grown in the fens. Meat counters in supermarkets show only beautifully cut pieces and there is no sign now of the carcasses that would be hung on display in the butchers' shops of old. A more direct link with agriculture might be found in the description given to, for example, 'farm fresh eggs', but as these may well have been produced in a commercial battery unit, the reality does not quite correspond to the image created by the label. Rather confusingly, those that are described as 'barn eggs', which might make one think of battery sheds, are produced in a slightly more rural environment, as described in Chapter 4. In most cases, however, food is presented for sale in a manner that is convenient and attractive to the cook or consumer rather than by reference to its origins. There are some exceptions to this with, for example, premium products as mentioned later, but the main impression gained in a supermarket could well be of pre-washed vegetables and fully prepared meals for the microwave.

Another aspect that makes the farm seem rather remote from the foodstore is the lack of any seasonal change. Agriculture revolves so much around the changing seasons and yet in the shops everything seems to be on offer throughout the year and there is little if any difference between summer and winter. Apples are always available, at a time perhaps when the orchards may be only just coming into leaf or still being pruned. Even strawberries, that used to be such a summer speciality, can now be bought at any time. This seemingly constant bounty is made possible by being able to import fresh foods from around the world and also by storing locally grown produce.

Shoppers now expect to be able to buy fresh produce all the year round and this facility is of course available thanks to modern means of transporting goods from more southerly parts of Europe and the rest of the world. What is perhaps less logical is that so many items seem to be imported from neighbouring countries even though they are being produced locally as well. The sight of bacon from Denmark or butter from Ireland, when there are so many cows and pigs to be seen in the British countryside, does confuse the connection that might otherwise be made between food on the shelves and the farms outside. The question of imports, whether from Europe or from other parts of the world, is complex and raises a number of issues that are outside the scope of this book. For the present purpose, it is mentioned just in the context of being one of the reasons why it can be difficult to link food in the shops to the farming industry that produces it.

Advances are, however, being made in establishing an origin or identity for certain foods as they are offered for sale. Organic products are separately labelled and attract a particular demand. This may not mean that the buyers of these goods then necessarily understand fully the practice behind organic farming, but it does create a connection between the consumer and the way in which the food is grown. There are other such categories too, such as Freedom Foods which is administered by the RSPCA and indicates that the animals have enjoyed a certain standard of welfare. Many of the supermarket chains now have a policy of sourcing food locally whenever feasible and the National Farmers Union (NFU) has introduced a symbol of a red tractor to show when food has been produced in Britain. There are also a number of trade organisations that market food as being of a particular origin, such as

Welsh Lamb or English Apples and Pears. All these serve to make the buyer more aware of where, and how, their food has been produced. Although supermarkets now handle the vast majority of food being sold in this country, and have effectively eclipsed the traditional butchers, grocers and green grocers, there are a growing number of new outlets that have a more direct link with the land from which the food is grown. These include the expanding range of farmers' markets as well as farm shops, Pick Your Own enterprises and Internet selling.

Not all farm produce goes to the retail market, in whichever form, and much is destined for wholesale, whether for catering or processing. The connection between these products and the farms on which they have been grown can be even more remote, be it in a smart restaurant or a factory canteen or even when someone is spooning out cat food!

10 DIVERSIFICATION

Diversification has become quite a buzz-word around the country and indeed its effect is easy to see in many areas. There are a number of factors behind this relatively recent revolution.

Falling farm incomes and the change in attitudes to agricultural production has inevitably encouraged farmers and landowners to look at alternative uses for their properties. Even if a farm is still being run profitably and to full capacity, there may be areas such as old buildings that are no longer properly useable for agriculture and which have therefore been converted to some other purpose. Also, as farms have become more specialised, there are buildings and land that have been vacated and are available for another, more lucrative, venture. An arable farm that traditionally would have had integrated within it a beef or dairy herd might now have given over the old livestock buildings and permanent pastures to an equestrian enterprise.

A growing demand for such facilities has been instrumental in creating diversification. Bed and breakfast accommodation and other tourist or leisure activities have been attracting an increasing number of visitors, especially in the more popular holiday regions. More recently, small businesses have found that their office or factory needs might be more pleasantly fulfilled in a rural environment.

Planning policies have also reflected the change in agricultural circumstances. Previously, while food production was still a national priority, there was a presumption against using good farmland for development. Latterly, this rule has been relaxed and allowing an alternative use would now often be seen as bringing new resources to a rural area. Even cherished landmarks such as stone barns are being imaginatively converted into residential and commercial units, whereas earlier planning policies would have been inclined against such alterations even though there was no viable means of maintaining them still in their former state.

Generally, however, the developer is required to retain the original features and it is indeed still possible to see what the traditional functions of a building would have been. The house or office that has a large central wall area faced with windows or encased with weatherboarding was probably the old tithe barn where the corn was brought for threshing in the draught created by two massive central doors. The livery stables with loose-boxes surrounding a central yard would previously have been a calfhouse or cowshed, where milking was done by hand and then perhaps with portable units. Some schemes are indeed still closely integrated with the farm business itself, such as the farm shop or visitor centre or Pick Your Own venture.

Another very visible change as farms become diversified is that the new activities are often advertised, either through the name of a company occupying the converted buildings being posted up by the entrance way, or by billboards. There has been a proposal to make it easier for planning authorities to allow such boards to be erected, so that this changing pattern could become even more noticeable. This is a considerable contrast to the traditional farming landscape where there has been little need to draw any attention to a property or the business being carried out there, other than perhaps a modest sign giving the name of the farm.

10 D I V E R S I F I C A T I O N

Although farms can be seen as isolated units in relatively remote locations, some are within villages where they would have been an important part of the local life, as an employer and provider of fresh milk and other produce. That role has now changed and the farmyard faces two new pressures: firstly, from the fact that land within a village is in much demand for housing; and secondly, that a working farm may be too noisy or smelly for modern villagers who have moved to the country for rural peace and not for the sound of tractors or grain driers or the smell of manure or silage! Such farmyards are now likely to be redeveloped for housing, with a replacement set of buildings then being erected on a site outside the village. This can explain why one might see a completely new farmyard at a time of recession when such an investment would not otherwise be expected.

Most diversification has taken place around the buildings rather than on the land, as the latter will generally be useable for farming under most conditions, in that it does not get outdated like a building which may be too low or narrow for modern machinery. Also, buildings are more readily put to alternative commercial uses, whereas open land is less adaptable. One striking exception to this is seen in golf courses, many of which will have been created on farmland and where it is now often difficult to picture how it would previously have looked when still under crops or grazing. It is difficult also to see how it could be converted back to farming were the economic and social balance between leisure and food production ever to change, what with the special grass and drainage of the greens and the bunkers and landscaped trees.

Some diversification schemes may have been sold on to third parties and so no longer involve the farmers on whose property they have been developed. In many cases, however, the introduction of a new venture has necessitated farmers acquiring new skills and attitudes. The growing of new types of crops, such as herbs or bio-mass, will require different techniques to those learnt for the cultivation of wheat or barley, as well as a new attitude to marketing. Most conventional farm crops have always

10 DIVERSIFICATION

been sold to some central buying organisation, whether in the form of a marketing board or a big firm of merchants. New types of produce for which there is as yet only a rather specialised market will need a more proactive approach. Some non-agricultural schemes such as farm shops or driving ranges will involve direct selling to the public, which few farmers will have done before, other than possibly with a few eggs or potatoes.

Other instances of rural diversification have only a remote link to farming, such as former airfields being used for industrial storage or Sunday markets and flooded gravel pits that are now stocked with fish for anglers. Quarrying for sand or gravel can have a major impact on the landscape, as deep pits are excavated and the spoil is transported away in heavy lorries. In some cases, however, the site can be refilled with municipal waste and restored to farmland. When completed, there will be little sign of any earlier disturbance, except perhaps for some tell-tale vents for the methane that builds up underground and has to be burnt off, causing a rather unreal sight after dark of blue flames flickering in the rural night.

11 CURRENT TRENDS AND FUTURE CHANGES

Organic Farming

Beautiful as the image of the countryside may be, there is something unappealing or even menacing about the sight of a sprayer working across an arable crop and seemingly drenching it with chemicals. There is increasing awareness and concern too about the thought of livestock being kept in close confinement or treated with powerful antibiotics. In practice, as has been mentioned earlier, such measures may not be quite as insensitive as they appear, but an alternative system does exist and one may wonder why it is not being more widely used. Organic farming has certainly become more commonplace in recent years and its products are now readily recognised and available, even if still at premium prices over conventionally grown food.

The principle behind organic production is that crops should be grown from sustainable farming systems that avoid the use of artificial ingredients such as fertilisers and pesticides. Livestock must be reared on feed produced by organic methods, without the use of chemical medication and be kept in humane conditions. These principles require a method of management that is quite different to modern conventional farming and it might be expected that the land on which they are being practised would look different too. In fact, there are no obvious signs to indicate that a farm is organic and, indeed, because of the skills and management time involved, it could well be that only part of a farm has organic status, alongside fields that are still being cultivated with artificial inputs. Certainly, the fact that no weedkillers are used does not mean that the land will be covered in colourful wild flowers, as the crops themselves still have to be nurtured and protected even if by non-chemical means such as hoeing, composting and the use of rotations.

Perhaps some clues might be found in what is *not* seen on the farm, such as a sprayer at work or the presence of an enclosed piggery or poultry house. Livestock are less intensively grazed than under normal methods, not on account of welfare considerations, but due to the more limited growth of grass when using only natural manuring processes. Similarly, arable crops give lighter yields than when fertilised and sprayed artificially and this, together with the greater management required, results in a higher price being required for the end product. The fact that organic foods depend on gaining a premium price creates a limitation on the amount that can be grown for the commercial markets. There are also situations where, due perhaps to the nature or location of the land, crops or livestock may be particularly vulnerable to certain infections that would be difficult to control with purely organic methods. This system of farming does in any event require a special skill and extra input of time.

The founding movement of organic farming in this country was the Soil Association, which has for years determined the standards under which produce may achieve a recognised organic status. Its rather unlikely name does emphasise the fact that successful organic production depends essentially upon being able to manage the soil as much as the crops or livestock. The land has to be worked in such a way so as to be able to sustain itself and not then require the application of artificial ingredients to replace whatever natural elements may have been removed by cropping. With the recent growth in this sector, it has gained the support of other specialised organisations such as Organic Farmers and Growers, as well as the Ministry of Agriculture.

The degree to which organic farming will continue to expand depends largely upon the number of consumers who are willing and able to pay premium prices for these products. Organic goods are likely to remain more expensive to produce than other foods due to the lower yields and higher management costs. Subsidies for this sector are provided only for the time required to convert from conventional farming, and not once full production is achieved, so that these higher costs have ultimately to be passed on to the consumer. Meanwhile, food safety standards are being constantly increased so that there will be a greater feeling of reassurance among the majority of the population about the quality of the ordinary food that they buy and less inclination or incentive to switch to organic produce.

11 CURRENT TRENDS AND FUTURE CHANGES

Integrated Farming

The visible distinction between organic and ordinary farms is not as great as it perhaps once was, due to the fact that the former have become increasingly efficient and so many of the latter do now also incorporate various environmental measures into their overall management. The presence of hedgerows and wild headlands or pockets of newly planted trees might fit the image of an organic system, but they could in fact be seen just as easily on a highly productive commercial farm. There are many incentives for taking more of an environmental approach, whether through grant aid, under for example the Countryside Stewardship Scheme, or through advice offered by government agencies. There are various means by which a better balance is sought by growers without having to take on all the strictures of an organic practice. Integrated Farming is one such method, in which management techniques are designed to allow a farm to remain highly productive whilst keeping artificial inputs to a minimum and preserving wildlife features.

Standards of Production

Another aspect of seeking to show that food has been produced in an acceptable manner is through standards imposed by the producers themselves. Where such methods have been adopted, the produce will be marketed under the relevant description, with examples being Farm Assured, Conservation Grade and the RSPCA welfare code. In each case, the crop is not expected to fulfil all the organic requirements but will have incorporated certain management practices on hygiene, welfare and conservation. These are intended to provide the consumer with a degree of reassurance and to give the product an additional appeal whilst still incorporating many of the ordinary commercial farming methods.

11 CURRENT TRENDS
AND FUTURE CHANGES

Genetically Modified Crops

There has been much debate about the use of genetically modified crops
and it is beyond the scope of this book to arbiter on the various issues
involved. In Britain, such crops are currently only grown on very limited
trial plots and even where those may be encountered there will be no visible
difference to a conventional crop of the same species. The rather dramatic
epithet of 'monster' or 'Frankenstein' that has been applied to them refers
rather extravagantly to the perceived principles by which they are created
rather than their actual appearance! In practical terms, the attraction of
modified crops is that they can be made to be resistant to certain diseases
and also tolerant of particular herbicides, so that fewer chemicals need be
used. They can also be provided with a protection against some forms of
natural decay, so that once harvested and processed they can be kept in
good condition for a longer period and incur less wastage. The impetus
behind this is essentially an economic one, arising from the lower cost of
making fewer chemical applications, although this would seemingly have
an environmental advantage too. The main concerns are, however, that it
is a new science that is not yet fully understood and that GM crops are
likely to cross-pollinate with conventional varieties and also wild plants.
That in turn could cause a spread of modified species that may become
uncontrollable due to their in-built resistance to conventional treatments.
These public perceptions and concerns mean that food retailers are being
expected to give assurances that the stock that they sell is GM-free, with the
result that they may then have to insist on a similar assurance from their
suppliers. Where that is the case, those farmers who might otherwise have
sought the commercial and other benefits of growing GM crops, might well
have to forsake them in favour of more conventional methods. Meanwhile,
in other parts of the world, notably in both North and South America, GM
crops are already being commercially grown, over a huge area apparently
now totalling around 100 million hectares. It will therefore be difficult in
Britain to avoid having consumer products that contain GMOs, especially

those containing soya which is a widely used source of protein that is only beginning to be grown successfully in this country and therefore depends extensively upon imports. This, and the fact that the American populations have been consuming GM products for some years without harm, may perhaps reduce the strength of feeling about such crops being used in Britain.

Global Warming

At one time, the concept of global warming conjured up images of Britain basking in a Mediterranean climate and crops such as oranges and almonds being grown here, while the southern part of Europe became more arid and less productive. More recently, however, it seems that the trend is towards wilder and wetter weather. If this were to become a regular phenomenon, the consequence to farmers would be manifold even in the short term. Arable cultivation is hampered by wet conditions, not only at harvest time when crops lose condition and become more expensive to gather in and to store, but also when carrying out the subsequent cultivations. New crops that are sown late or into wet and badly worked ground will develop less well than if the circumstances had allowed an earlier entry into a finer seedbed. Heavy and unseasonal rain can reduce the effectiveness of fertiliser and chemical applications. Where flooding is likely to occur, the newly sown crops might be washed away or damaged so that such land would have to be limited to spring crops or even to grazing. Flooding of grassland restricts the times at which the land can be safely used by livestock, but does not otherwise cause irreparable damage and, indeed, the river silt can add to the fertility of the land. Wetter conditions do, however, limit the period over which other pastures may be grazed, as the grass starts to grow later in the spring and is more likely to be damaged by livestock, especially in the autumn.

If there really were to be a steady increase in rainfall in Britain, then certain changes might occur in current farming practice. Some crops would

11 CURRENT TRENDS
AND FUTURE CHANGES

become too difficult to grow except in the most ideal situations, so that it might no longer be feasible to produce potatoes, for example, on land that has a slight clay content. The heavy yielding cereals that had until now produced the best economic returns may have to be replaced by varieties with stronger and shorter straw to avoid losses through 'lodging' or being beaten down. It could also become increasingly difficult to make hay of a sufficiently good quality, meaning that other forage crops would have to be grown instead. There may be one positive aspect for those growers who rely on irrigation, which has in the recent past been restricted in some areas due to declining water resources, but which would presumably by then be well replenished.

If such climate change were to continue for the longer term it would necessitate many other changes in the countryside, even to the extent of abandoning some coastal farmland areas. In the mean while, however, it is likely to be a case of accepting a rising cost in production, whether through grain drying or buying in feed, and also a reduction in quantity and quality and therefore in income.

Conservation

The modern concept of rural conservation has evolved from a number of factors. Firstly, the era of post-war food shortages in Britain and throughout much of continental Europe was replaced, due to expansive agricultural policies and techniques, by a period of general over-supply. This allowed society to take stock of how those increases in production had been achieved and, as they were no longer a political priority, to consider how a more natural environmental balance might be found. Meanwhile, too, the developed countries were expecting higher levels of welfare and enjoying a greater mobility so that more people could visit the countryside and become involved in it. Rural policies at both European and national levels have reflected this growing requirement for environmental measures.

171

11 CURRENT TRENDS AND FUTURE CHANGES

Public funding is being increasingly directed towards enhancing wildlife habitats and improving access, at the expense essentially of support for commercial farming. The indications are that such policies will continue to be implemented for the foreseeable future. We will therefore in all probability see more trees and hedges being planted, more paths and other facilities being created and more restrictions being imposed on some of the ways in which commercial farming and forestry are operated.

Access

Within this general approach to the countryside is also a requirement for improved public access to the countryside, whether along roads and paths or as a freedom to roam across open ground. Such facilities are likely to be developed further and in some cases become more formalised, possibly in conjunction with a visitor attraction. These may be quite noticeable in that they tend to be in popular sites, although their wider effect will be more a matter of the way in which the public then intrude on farming businesses rather than any significant visual impact. Some paths and open spaces will come under pressure from growing numbers of visitors and from the various ways in which they might use them, such as by horse or with cross-country vehicles. There will be increased pressure, too, on the roads and car parking requirements in the more popular areas. More 'pay as you go' bridleways may be created to help relieve some of these pressures, as well as scrambler tracks and cross-country driving courses. It would be nice to think that there might be some improvement in the process whereby outdated paths could be moved to alternative routes more suited to modern needs, but there is still little indication of any impending change in the current procedures.

11 CURRENT TRENDS AND FUTURE CHANGES

Diversification

Diversification, as mentioned in the previous chapter, has become increasingly evident over recent years and is bound to continue to impact on many areas of the countryside, with a greater emphasis on the more accessible and populated areas than in the remoter districts. Planning policies are now geared increasingly towards making it easier to convert old farm buildings or to set up new ventures on former agricultural property, and European funding will also continue to be earmarked for those rural areas where alternative developments are going to be needed. There is a limit, however, to the scale and range that such diversification is likely to reach, due to restrictions in market potential and in infrastructure.

Building Development

Farmland is the raw material for building development and with a population that is growing in number and in prosperity there is growing

pressure to build new houses and workplaces. In an effort to protect the countryside, there is currently a political preference towards redeveloping disused urban sites rather than 'green fields'. There are difficulties with this, regarding such issues as contamination and infrastructure, and there will therefore inevitably have to be more new construction in rural locations. This has disadvantages in that it will be seen as spoiling most peoples' perception of the countryside and create pressure upon limited roads and transport systems. On the other hand, it can be argued that such developments would bring a new prosperity to the country, although this will tend to focus on the more accessible areas and be of little consequence to the more remote districts where such added income would be more vital. Villages in accessible and sought-after areas are likely to be expanded, probably with high-density housing estates that cannot really reflect the space and expanse associated with a country area. Even with this new influx of people and resources, it seems unlikely that it would be feasible to make any significant improvement in public transport, so that the local lanes will have to absorb a car population that will have risen as rapidly as the human one. The need for every adult to have their own car introduces a financial threshold on who can afford to live in these villages. It is to be hoped that the efforts being made to create affordable homes or social housing will serve to retain a balance within rural communities, although the lack of local services and transport will mean that those without a car will become isolated.

Commercial and industrial development in rural areas will tend to be of a limited scale due to such factors as access and availability of staff and will also tend to be in the more populous locations.

Land Prices

As land is the basis of almost every farm business, one would expect that a decline in agricultural incomes would be reflected in a corresponding fall in the value of farmland. In fact, the national statistics show little evidence of

11 CURRENT TRENDS AND FUTURE CHANGES

this during recent years and, indeed, while farm incomes are recorded as having dropped by as much as 70% between 1995 and 2000, land prices showed a rise of over 30% over the same period. There are many reasons for this, including statistical anomalies and a great reluctance among farmers to sell their land particularly during a recession, but the main cause relates to the almost unique nature of the British countryside.

Being a relatively small and heavily populated island with a varied and attractive landscape, farmland in Britain attracts a wider range of interests than in most other countries. Land in the UK is not just a means of producing food, as it would be in, say, the Midwest of the United States where it is really only used for grain production and has little other appeal. Here, on the other hand, it may be bought for a variety of reasons, such as residential or amenity purposes, field sports or for development and diversification. In each of these cases, there is money coming into the countryside from sources that are unrelated to agriculture, whether from commercial and financial sectors or even from overseas, and this has served to boost values in many areas.

From a purely agricultural point of view, the value of land is likely to be determined to a large extent by its quality. There is, however, no ready measure of whether soils are good or bad, although there is a national system of classification which is often taken as being a yardstick for quality. This is recorded on a series of maps that cover the whole country and show five grades of land (or 'classes' in Scotland). The implication is that Grade 1 is of the best quality and that Grade 5 is the worst, and indeed, advertisements and particulars of farms for sale may well make reference to this classification as a selling feature if the land happens to be in one of the top grades. However, the system was devised essentially as a measure of the versatility of land rather than its quality, in order to assist planning authorities in determining which areas should be retained for agriculture rather than being built over. Grade 1 land is therefore of a type that can be used for the widest range of crops, such as vegetables, bulbs and roots, whilst Grade 3

11 CURRENT TRENDS
AND FUTURE CHANGES

would be restricted to combineable crops and Grade 4 is best left to pasture. The most versatile land, such as is found in the fens of the eastern counties, may well be of high quality, but is also associated with a highly specialised, and often risky, system of cropping and is not necessarily the 'best' for every farmer. The majority of arable land in Britain was classified as Grade (or Class) 3 and this has since been subdivided with a category of 3a.

An indication of the changing role of agriculture within the country has been seen in a recent change in government policy relating to land classification. Previously, if a planning application were made on land that was classified as Grade 1, 2 or 3a, the local authority would be required to refer the case to the Ministry of Agriculture, Fisheries and Food. This provided effectively a curb on development of such high-calibre land, but local councils are now able to make their own decisions on these areas, which would imply that they are no longer to be considered to be an inalienable source of vital food production.

Agri-business

One response to falling agricultural incomes has been to improve efficiency through economies of scale. This is generally achieved by taking on more land, either by acquisition or through renting or contracting off neighbours. Farm businesses are therefore on average getting larger and fewer in number, although this is not necessarily going to have a particularly noticeable effect on the landscape. The trend of earlier years when such expansion resulted in the removal of hedges and the construction of big new buildings is now reversed. Even the most commercial farm business is now subject to environmental regulations and incentives. Field sizes are unlikely therefore to increase significantly, although the machinery working on them will often be larger than that used in the past, as the bigger farm units exploit the advantage of scale and as more of the smaller farmers find it expedient to use contractors.

11 CURRENT TRENDS AND FUTURE CHANGES

Silage being made in a clamp

Larger farms require the highest standards of management and are more likely to have the resources to use the most modern commercial techniques. Previously this would have led to a greater use of chemicals and a more ruthless management of the land. Modern practices have, however, been changing and, in agricultural terms, big is not necessarily unbeautiful. The enlargement of farm business whether by ownership or leasing or through greater use of co-operatives may in fact result in more tree planting in field corners or bigger and more permanent areas of setaside, rather than in any increase in 'prairie' farming.

Rural Communities

The trend over the last 50 years or so has been a decline in the number of farmers and a rise in their average age. The agricultural community has become polarised, with some farms becoming larger and highly

177

11 CURRENT TRENDS AND FUTURE CHANGES

commercial and others remaining more traditional and now often part-time. Within that is also a middle ground of family farms and diversified enterprises. Those working in forestry are also much reduced in number and dependent upon commercial management and contracting companies rather than on individual owners such as the big estates. Many others who worked alongside these businesses, such as gamekeepers and blacksmiths, have inevitably followed the same trend. Meanwhile, villages have expanded and absorbed an increasingly diverse population, most of whom may well have come from an urban environment and have no direct link with the land. The farming community that used to predominate in almost all rural areas does so now in only the more remote districts. Elsewhere, other interests have filled some, but not all, of the aspects of country life. There is perhaps a parallel with some coastal villages that 100 years ago would have been largely dependent upon fishing, but which have since then seen their commercial and social life being replaced by tourism, marinas, retirement homes and other related services and businesses. There is a further parallel in that both farmers and fishermen believe that they provide an essential product in the form of food and that their industries are therefore indispensable. The difference with the countryside as opposed to the sea is that it is the farmers who still maintain the landscape that surrounds and in many ways sustains the new communities. A further factor is that the process of change is still occurring and indeed still accelerating.

Under current planning policies there is a preference for new development to take place within or around urban areas rather than on 'greenfield' sites, but there is inevitably in many areas an ongoing loss of farmland for new building. This has not only a visual impact on the landscape but also contributes to the tide of change in the countryside, arising from the increase in housing and new businesses and services. Meanwhile, the emphasis of agricultural policy is switching away from providing financial support for the production of food and is increasingly focused on environmental issues, through both regulation and grant aid. As a result, farmers are having to take an increasingly commercial approach to their

11 CURRENT TRENDS AND FUTURE CHANGES

core business of agriculture, whilst at the same time working within the regulations and incentives that govern other aspects of the land, such as conservation and public access. The forestry industry will also be driven increasingly by similar regulations and incentives aimed more at fulfilling environmental aspirations than commercial returns.

In farming, the ongoing need for efficiency will result in fewer people working on the land and in the use of larger machinery and of the most economical production methods. This may lead to some farmsteads being taken out of agriculture and others being expanded with new buildings. It will probably also mean that modern scientific developments will have to be introduced, such as in the use of GM crops and increasingly sophisticated pesticides, as otherwise British and European farmers would become unable to compete within the world markets. Serious as these commercial pressures and hardening regulations may be for the businesses of farming and forestry, they are unlikely to wreak any equivalent change upon the landscape itself, as environmental issues are now such a fundamental part of rural policy. We may not therefore see a repeat of the loss of hedgerows and rationalisation of farming practices that accompanied the drive for increased efficiency in the post-war period. Let us hope, however, that there will not be instead a return to the time of the pre-war recession when farming was under such pressure that many areas of land became derelict.

12 EPILOGUE

Images that Formed Our Present Landscape

The image that I have before me when I think of how our landscape has been formed during the last century is, strangely, of smokestacks. Smokestacks as much of battleships as of factories, for it was the need to keep a navy supplied with coal that has created our present-day forestry industry and the threat from naval attack that revolutionised the nation's farming policy.

Indeed, even before the First World War, shipping had an impact on forestry that is still seen today. At one time, of course, ships were built of timber and our native broadleaved woods provided the oak with which they were constructed. When, however, ships began to be made of iron and steel, there was less demand for oak and less incentive to replant or plan for the future. These new vessels then wrought another, rather unexpected, change to the nation's forests; as they were driven now no longer by wind but by steam, they needed reliable stocks of coal for fuel and this was transported out and bunkered around the world. Having made their deliveries, the supply ships would return to Britain for a further load, sailing as often as not empty of any cargo. Not only was this uneconomic, but also unsafe and in order to give the necessary stability they would carry ballast, which would often be of valueless stone. Then, from some parts of the world, it became feasible to take on board as ballast a load of timber which could be sold upon return. With cheap imported timber being dumped, almost literally, onto the UK market, prices fell and the longer term management of many of the country's woods and forests suffered as a result. Since our native hardwoods take over 100 years to mature, the effects of this policy can still be seen today.

At that time, Britain was a heavily industrialised nation and most of the factories relied on coal as their source of energy. This became particularly crucial during the First World War when the production of armaments made rising demands on manufacturing. Coal mines in turn relied upon a ready supply of pit props which were hewn from timber, often at a semi-mature stage. As a result, by the end of the war, the countryside was seriously depleted of timber and the Government of the day established the Forestry Commission with the purpose essentially of ensuring that these commercial stocks would be replenished. This involved a greater emphasis on faster growing conifers than would traditionally have been the case. In the event, another war within only 20 years caused a further reduction in timber resources so that thereafter there was an even greater rationale for growing conifers. The outcome of this policy can be still seen quite starkly in the form of regimented blocks of conifers being grown around the country and especially in the uplands of Scotland and Wales.

Battleships form the image of the farming landscape too. By the time of the Second World War, Britain relied heavily on being able to import not only exotic but also basic foodstuffs. This was brought in by sea and the supplies were of course seriously endangered by enemy action. Food became scarce and was still being rationed many years after the end of the war. Understandably, one of the first priorities in peace time was to increase domestic food production and new laws and subsidies were introduced to encourage farmers and landowners towards this. The industry responded with new techniques and bigger machines, leading to visible changes in the landscape as hedges were grubbed out to rationalise fields or large asbestos-clad buildings were erected. Even during the war, old pastures had been ploughed up so as to enable more crops to be grown and would then often have been left in arable cultivation thereafter. Before all this, farming had been in a serious recession that was really only reversed by the outbreak of war and the desperate need for home-produced food. The memory of that recession would still have been in everyone's mind when the new post-war policies and practices were being devised.

My next image is of the 15 gold stars that encircle the blue flag of the European Union. When the UK joined the European Economic Community in 1973, farmers continued to enjoy political and financial support but for

12 EPILOGUE

different reasons to those of 30 years before. The Common Agricultural Policy was aimed only partly at maintaining a strategic level of food production and otherwise at sustaining viable rural communities throughout the Community. For many years this continued to be based almost entirely on the amount of crops grown or numbers of animals reared and the countryside continued to be exploited accordingly and to contribute to the notorious mountains and lakes of surplus foodstuffs. Alongside this image it would now be appropriate to add the symbol of the World Trade Organisation through which new international initiatives are being taken to reduce subsidised over-production, leading also to changes in countryside management.

This introduces my final image, which is of a butterfly. It is one of many symbols that could be chosen to represent not just the fragility of nature but also the growing interest within Britain and much of the developed world for the environment and conservation. This interest is then incorporated into national and international policies which result, on the one hand, in restrictive regulations being imposed but also, on the other hand, in new financial resources being made available. We seem now to care more for the butterfly than for butter and this is beginning to be reflected in the landscape, as we see a growing number of tree guards and wild areas and fewer cows. These environmental concerns have been extended also to cover broader issues of conscience and opinion, such as animal welfare, public access, and the use of chemicals and other scientific advances. Not all of these are directly visible in the overall appearance of the landscape but each one does impinge on the very fabric of the countryside. Some of them erode the old traditions that have been such an important part of rural life and will therefore also cause loss and hardship to the individuals who have sustained those traditions, but others bring a new and potentially attractive impetus. Few would argue, for example, with the growth of organic farming, provided that it is sustainable, but others will regret the closure of the local livestock market or the dismantling of a family farm as it is merged into a bigger, impersonal business.

12 EPILOGUE

The old traditions and the modern methods of farming and forestry have both been founded on well-practised expertise. New regulations are often devised in response to well-meaning but possibly ill-informed opinion and as a consequence they may fail to produce the required result. For example, insisting on the planting of only broadleaved trees may seem a direct way of reversing the earlier spread of conifer plantations, except that in practice the two need to be mixed if one is to end up with a successful stand of oak or beech. Also, do those who hark back to the image of natural woods really want to have only deciduous trees and not see any greenery in our woods throughout the winter months?

It is frustrating when even well-intentioned opinions such as those just mentioned result in a counterproductive outcome, but not all such opinions are particularly well meant. Do we now as a nation really care more for the plight of foxes than of farmers?

FURTHER READING

184

Bell, B. *Farm Machinery* Farming Press 1999.

Blake, F. *Organic Farming and Growing* Crowood Press 1994.

Boatfield, G. *Farm Livestock* Farming Press 1994.

Carter, E.S. and Stansfield, J.M. *British Farming. Changing Policies and Production Systems* Farming Press 1994.

Department of the Environment, Transport and the Regions. *Our Countryside: The Future* DETR 2000.

Hibberd, B.G. (ed) *Forestry Practice* Forestry Commission 1991.

Hobson, J.C.J. *Gamekeeping* The Crowood Press 1994.

Lambkin, N. *Organic Farming* Farming Press 1999.

Mitchell, A. *The Pocket Guide to Trees* Dragon's World 1990.

Ritson, C. and Harvey, D.R. (eds). *The Common Agricultural Policy* CAB International 1997.

Soffe R.J. (ed) *The Agricultural Notebook* Blackwell Science 1995.

COUNTRYSIDE ORGANISATIONS
AND SOURCES OF FURTHER INFORMATION

Association of Show and Agricultural Organisations
The Showground, Shepton Mallett, Somerset BA4 6QN
Tel: 01749 822200

Council for the Protection of Rural England
Warwick House, 25 Buckingham Palace Road, London SW1W OPP
Tel: 020 7976 6433
www.cpre.org.uk

Country Landowners Association
16 Belgrave Square, London SW1X 8PQ
Tel: 020 7235 0511 *(and regional representation)*
www.cla.org.uk

The Countryside Agency
John Dower House, Crescent Place, Cheltenham GL50 3RA
Tel: 01242 521381 *(and regional representation)*
www.countryside.gov.uk

The Countryside Alliance
The Old Town Hall, 367 Kennington Road, London SE11 4PT
Tel: 020 7840 9200
www.countryside-alliance.org

Department of the Environment, Transport and the Regions
Eland House, Bressenden Place, London SW1E 5DU
Tel: 020 7944 3000 *(and regional representation)*
www.detr.gov.uk

English Nature
Northminster House, Northminster, Peterborough PE1 1UA
Tel: 01733 455000 *(and regional representation)*
www.english-nature.org.uk

COUNTRYSIDE ORGANISATIONS
AND SOURCES OF FURTHER INFORMATION

Farmers Union of Wales

Llys Amaeth, Plas Gorgerddon, Aberystwyth SY23 3BT

Tel: 01970 820 820820

Farmers Weekly

Quadrant House, The Quadrant, Sutton SM2 5AS

Tel: 020 8652 4005

www.fwi.co.uk

Food and Farming Education Services

National Agricultural Centre, Stoneleigh Park

Kenilworth CV8 2LZ

Tel: 0246 858259

www.foodandfarming.org

Food From Britain

123 Buckingham Palace Road, London SW1W 9SA

Tel: 020 7233 5111

Forestry Commission

231 Corstorphine Road, Edinburgh EH12 7AT

Tel: 0131 334 0303 (*and regional representation*)

www.forestry.gov.uk

Ministry of Agriculture, Fisheries and Food

Noble House, 17 Smith Square, London SW1A 2HH

Tel: 0645 335577 (*and regional representation*)

www.maff.gov.uk

National Agricultural Centre

Stoneleigh Park, Kenilworth CV8 2LZ

Tel: 024 7669 6969

COUNTRYSIDE ORGANISATIONS
AND SOURCES OF FURTHER INFORMATION

National Farmers Union (NFU)
Agriculture House, 164 Shaftesbury Avenue, London WC2H 8HL
Tel: 020 7331 7200
www.nfu.org.uk

National Farmers Union of Scotland
Rural Centre, West Mains, Ingleston, Newbridge EH28 8LT
Tel: 0131 472 4000

National Federation of Young Farmers Clubs
YFC Centre, National Agricultural Centre, Stoneleigh Park
Kenilworth CV8 2LZ
Tel: 01203 696544
www.yfc-web.org.uk

National Parks Council
246 Lavender Hill, London SW11 1LJ
Tel: 020 7924 4077

National Trust
36 Queen Anne's Gate, London SW1H 9AS
Tel: 020 7222 9251
www.nationaltrust.org.uk

NFU Countryside
Agriculture House, North Gate, Uppingham, Rutland LE15 9PL
Tel: 01572 824220
www.nfucountryside.org.uk

Organic Farmers and Growers Ltd
Churchgate House, 50 High Street, Soham, Ely CB7 5HF
Tel: 01844 279352

COUNTRYSIDE ORGANISATIONS
AND SOURCES OF FURTHER INFORMATION

Ramblers Association

87-90 Albert Embankment, London, SE1 7TW

Tel: 020 7339 8500

www.ramblers.org.uk

Scottish Office

Agriculture, Environment and Fisheries Department

Pentland House, 47 Robbs Loan, Edinburgh EH14 1TY

Tel: 0131 556 8400

Scottish Natural Heritage

12 Hope Terrace, Edinburgh EH9 2AS

Tel: 0131 447 4784

Soil Association

Bristol House, 40-56 Victoria Street, Bristol BS1 6BY

Tel: 0117 929 0661

www.soilassociation.org.uk

Welsh Office

Agriculture Department, Crown Buildings

Cathays Park, Cardiff CF2 1UY

Tel: 01222 825111

www.wales.gov.uk

INDEX

INDEX